A STUDENT'S GUIDE TO
THE STUDY OF LAW

THE PRESTON A. WELLS JR.
GUIDES TO THE MAJOR DISCIPLINES

AMERICAN POLITICAL THOUGHT *George W. Carey*

CLASSICS *Bruce S. Thornton*

THE CORE CURRICULUM *Mark C. Henrie*

ECONOMICS *Paul Heyne*

INTERNATIONAL RELATIONS *Angelo M. Codevilla*

LIBERAL LEARNING *James V. Schall, S.J.*

LITERATURE *R. V. Young*

MUSIC HISTORY *R. J. Stove*

NATURAL SCIENCE *Stephen M. Barr*

PHILOSOPHY *Ralph M. McInerny*

POLITICAL PHILOSOPHY *Harvey C. Mansfield*

PSYCHOLOGY *Daniel N. Robinson*

RELIGIOUS STUDIES *D. G. Hart*

STUDY OF HISTORY *John Lukacs*

U.S. HISTORY *Wilfred M. McClay*

A Student's Guide to the Study of Law

GERARD V. BRADLEY

WITH A BIBLIOGRAPHIC ESSAY
BY CORY L. ANDREWS

ISI BOOKS
WILMINGTON, DELAWARE

A Student's Guide to the Study of Law is made possible by grants from the Lee and Ramona Bass Foundation, the Lillian S. Wells Foundation, the Huston Foundation, Barre Seid Foundation, the Law Enforcement Legal Defense Fund, and the Wilbur Foundation. The Intercollegiate Studies Institute gratefully acknowledges their support.

Bradley, Gerard V., 1954–

    A student's guide to the study of law / Gerard V. Bradley ; with a bibliographical appendix by Cory L. Andrews. — 1st ed. — Wilmington, Del. : ISI Books, c2006.

        p. ; cm.
        (ISI guides to the major disciplines)

        ISBN-13: 978-1-882926-97-8 (pbk.)
        ISBN-10: 1-882926-97-8 (pbk.)
        Includes bibliographical references.

        1. Law—United States—History. 2. Law—United States—Study and teaching. 3. Law—United States—Philosophy. 4. Political science—United States. 5. Religion and law—United States. I. Title. II. Series.

KF385 .B73 2006   2006922011
349.73—dc22   0604

ISI Books
Intercollegiate Studies Institute
3901 Centerville Road
Wilmington, DE 19807
www.isibooks.org

Design by Sam Torode

CONTENTS

PREFACE

A STUDENT'S GUIDE TO THE STUDY OF LAW might sound like a basic rulebook, a guide to the regulations governing a college campus, such as disciplinary procedures or which "help" number to call if you are picked up for underage drinking. This guide is altogether a different matter, however. It is not for students in trouble, but for those who wish to really understand the civil law of a political society such as the United States.

This slim volume focuses on matters that most law schools neglect, or teach badly, or both. Undergraduate law courses, or even graduate programs in legal philosophy, are little better. Outside the academy—in popular culture and in ambient political debate—it is also hard to get a reliable grip on the issues. This guide concentrates on what you need to know to really understand civil law but cannot easily find elsewhere.

"Really understand" sounds like one of those diaphanous phrases professors throw around like confetti. Not in this case. Part of what I mean by it is conveyed by the following anecdote: A mother asked her son after his first day of law school, "So, honey, how many *laws* did you learn today?" She expected that, on a good day, her son would bring home information such as how many directors it takes to make a corporation, or that the president's term is four years, or that felonies are crimes punishable by more than a year in prison. That is not what learning law is really about, however, as it ignores the distinction between the information content of the legal system—so many *laws*—and *law* as a rich concept of how to order life in society. One can't know *law* without knowing some *laws*, lest one be stuck trying to understand a ghost, or a null set. But *law* involves a lot more than the aggregate of all the *laws* one can memorize. Just think of the difference between facts about what happened a long time ago, and history as you learn it (or ought to learn it) in college or graduate school.

A Student's Guide to the Study of Law is therefore not a compendium of laws. If you want to know what the rule against perpetuities is, or what one has to do to commit the crime of burglary in the third degree, look elsewhere: consult the standard reference works readily available to the practitioner, Google "burglary" and see what comes up, or enroll in law school. Law schools convey *what* the law is pretty effectively: they communicate the rules, statutes, decisions, and other verbal expressions of the positive law pretty well. But law schools do a poor job transmitting law's moral foundations: they do not teach very well where law comes from, what it is *for*, and how to morally judge it. These are the "moral foundations of law" and are essential to a true understanding of the subject. And that is what this book is about.

This focus on "moral foundations" is not for high-flyers only—the overachievers destined for professional heights—but rather for anyone. Undergraduates studying law, curious students in other disciplines, and ordinary citizens trying to articulate their views on same-sex "marriage," or capital punishment, or the exclusion of "under God" in the Pledge of Allegiance: *all* can find their bearings in this book.

The foundational guidance every law student needs comprises two things. One is the conviction that law *has* foundations in objective morality. The other is a primer on the complex relationship between law and morality. Anyone possessed of both is equipped to tackle a lifetime of morally loaded challenges to the law, a menu of problems we see now only through a glass darkly, if we see them at all. Engendering that conviction and supplying that basic understanding are the objectives of this guide.

Understanding law and morality is not a mechanistic process. It involves some simple principles, but it is not akin to a simple equation or set of rules. Among other things, it is necessary to understand the moral truth that law is for persons—not the other way around—and the fact that no one has ever proposed that civil law simply reproduce morality. (More on these two propositions in chapter 1 and appendix E, respectively.) Understanding principles such as these is a necessary start—no more, no less—to getting law and morality right.

Morality and law do not follow a straight path, navigable once the autopilot is engaged, but instead follow a path more like that of a sailing vessel on a long and difficult journey. Basic principles are essential: sailors get lost without a compass heading, navigation skills, or knowledge of how a sailboat works. But sailors need more than that to get where they want to go. They have to respond to the sea and wind and weather conditions at hand, relying upon fundamental principles but creatively adapting them, tacking to and fro as they go. And it takes a captain's mastery to get through the most challenging situations.

Morality and law are mutually engaged along a course that winds through a political society's life. Sometimes the relationship is clean and simple, governed by straightforward principles. At other times it is a complex mix of contingencies, and it takes a master's feel to get the matter right. No treatment of the relationship could be exhaustive; there are always new challenges calling forth creative responses to perennial principles. My intention here is to walk the reader through some of the difficult turnings on the path of law studies, and to show what some of the heavily traveled intersections of law and morality look like. This guide includes some thick descriptions of problem areas and contested terrain. Its method is often illustrative.

Chapter 1 looks at the extralegal moral realities—human persons and their communities—that law is intended to serve. It examines how U.S. law over the last generation or so has diverted law from the moral realities it is supposed to support. Our law now prizes consensus more than it does serving its true purposes.

Chapter 2 explores the pathways linking law to the surrounding culture and conventional morality. It also navigates the bramble patch of law's "double" life. The prickly thing is that law is both *prescriptive*—a source of norms telling people what they ought to do—and *descriptive*, capable of being reported, with no normative import, as simply the say-so of some distant body of legislators or judges. Safety lies not in denying one or the other of law's "lives," but in integrating the two into a coherent understanding of law as both cultural artifact and moral norm.

Chapter 3 examines the role of religion and its relation to objective morality in our constitutional order. Finally, chapter 4 concerns the most practically important area of law: crime and punishment, the stuff of every other television program these days. In addition, there are six explanatory appendices to augment and further illustrate the arguments included in the text.

INTRODUCTION

A LITTLE MORE THAN A HUNDRED years ago Oliver Wendell Holmes Jr. dedicated the new Boston University law building. Holmes would soon be named to the United States Supreme Court, where he would serve as an associate justice for thirty years. On that festive day in 1897 he already was a member of Massachusetts' highest court, a renowned legal scholar, and halfway through a career that would make him the most important figure in American legal history. He urged Boston's law students to get "to the bottom of the subject." He promised them that, by concentrating on the more general aspects of law, each would "not only become a great master in [his] calling, but connect [the] subject with the universe and catch an echo of the infinite, a glimpse of its unfathomable process, a hint of the universal law."[1]

Holmes was right: "masters" of the law *do* grasp its essential underpinnings—what Holmes called "theory"—without sacrificing attention to detail. He opined that any "competent" student could do both. Holmes hit another of his marks, too: the "bottom" of civil law *does* connect to "universal law." But Holmes was profoundly mistaken about what that "universal" law is about.

Holmes well knew that popular morality and religious faith had much to do with the law of his day. He knew that many lawyers, too, believed in objective morality and traditional religious doctrine. But Holmes had left his religious faith behind on Civil War battlefields, where he was thrice wounded. He famously derided the notion of a universal moral law as the supernaturalist's fable, or as "a brooding omnipresence in the sky," the individual's fancy that what he could not help believing was somehow woven into the fabric of the world. And he wanted very much to uproot the whole moralistic vision of law that surrounded him.

Holmes knew that the first step needed to change the law was to change how people understood the law. And what better group to evangelize than Boston's law students? Holmes boldly presented to them his idea of the "man of the future"—"the man of statistics and the master of economics." Holmes wanted lawyers to be men—and women—of tomorrow, not yesterday or today. These "new" lawyers would be oracles; they would see the way law should be understood. They would then become reformers; they would *make* law as it should be made.

Holmes was no mean prophet. For him and for many since, the social sciences, chiefly economics, form the baseline foundation, the "bottom" of law. Today, many theorists who count Holmes as their forebear see at law's "bottom" even harder behavioral sciences, such as sociobiology and other disciplines which explain human behavior on the basis of mechanistic assumptions that implicitly deny human free choice. For these behaviorists, cause and effect is the complete explanation of human behavior. It is all in the hard wiring: people cannot do other than they do. Based on these suppositions, morality cannot be the foundation of law because there is no reality to morality. What's the point of deciding what is right and wrong about human choices, if people cannot choose at all?

The real challenge of the future—today as much as when Holmes dedicated the law building—has to do with moral truths that are not reducible to calculus, with propositions concerning right and wrong that do not fit on utility curves. At law's "bottom" lies the domain of objective morality, the critical standards by which one judges what one (or another) decides (or has decided) to do to be either morally upright or morally vicious. These moral norms are antecedent to all human choosing. They do not depend for their soundness upon custom or culture. Their validity does not depend upon human approbation. They do not depend upon their reception into the positive law for their truth. They are norms justified by their rational force, by their reasonableness, by their truth—and not by their conformity to the law of averages. Positive law supervenes upon this domain. Its distinctive contribution to morality takes the form of directing people's action in political community towards justice.

This does not mean, of course, that all laws are morally justified, any more than Holmes meant that all laws would some day actually make economic sense. Laws are made by fallible human beings, all too susceptible to flattery and corruption and prejudice. Legal systems will always be mixtures, more or less, of truth and error, wisdom and folly. But human finitude is no excuse for denying that law is to be understood as an extension or special case of ethics.

One cannot understand law save by its connection to objective moral ends. One can make no more sense of law as ordered to iniquity than one can of religion as ordered to money or power or rationalization. Part of the empirical story about religion involves venality, betrayal, and falls from grace. But religion itself has to do with the transcendent. The history of legal systems includes plenty of derailments into injustice. But law itself is about good order in political society—and that is how one has to see it if one is to see it clearly at all.

1. WHAT LAW IS *FOR*:
PERSONS AND THEIR COMMUNITIES
ॐ

THE SUBJECT MATTER of this guide is *positive* law: what human authorities have enacted or laid down—and in that sense *posited*—to order the common affairs of people living in political society. So habituated are we to living under law, and so ubiquitous is praise for the rule of law, that we forget that law is a recent invention, one with a very special appeal. This is not to suggest that before law there was universal chaos. It is to say that law is one of many methods by which to establish and maintain social order—and a latecomer, at that.

For millennia, societies were governed not by impartial and general requirements binding ruler and ruled alike, but by the ukase or *dictat* of the powerful one. Sometimes what were thought to be divine directives took precedence; other times the wise man dispensed justice while seated serenely under a date palm. Custom, or what was said to be the way of the ancestors, supplied additional principles of order in many societies. Perhaps in most places most of the time, order was achieved through a complex blend of all these authoritative sources. But none of these kinds of order is much like legal order, as we shall shortly see.

Law takes its place beside other kinds of order even in our society. Custom governs much of our social interaction. We do as we do in our families and in our friendships and on our sports teams because of what is expected and valued by others, not because it is written in the state's law. Huge companies are run on managerial principles that do not value, as law does, incremental change that is widely debated before it is implemented, and then implemented only with plenty of advance notice. This does not mean that corporations are beyond the law. They are not. Employees are protected by the civil law against sexual harassment, for example, and against dismissal in retaliation for union activity. But, in today's economy more than ever, corporate managers need to turn on a dime and act quickly. Legislators operate at a more leisurely pace, and so there are differences between managerial ways of governance and political ways of governance. Military governance is different still. Armies are governed (in part) by civil law (at least, our military is, since it is under civilian control). Armies are also governed (in part) as management would run a global corporation. But an army is *distinctively* governed by command authority, which looks and works very differently from legal and simple managerial authority. Furthermore, some churches and other voluntary associations are run by charismatic figures whose say-so has the same effect as that of a palm-tree caliph. None of these operate as our legal system operates.

The positive law of political society was "discovered" by Thomas Aquinas, the great medieval philosopher. Though there were legal codes as far back as Old Testament times, Aquinas first proposed that human law formed a distinct subject matter worth studying in its own right. He saw that law is a distinctive way of ordering social interaction. He recognized, too, that even though positive law was a man-made thing, it was brought into existence to serve moral purposes that man did not create. Positive law was *for* purposes external to itself. As the world's leading natural law theorist, Oxford legal philosopher John Finnis writes, "[t]here are human goods that can be secured only through the institutions of human law, and requirements of practical reasonableness which only those institutions can satisfy."[2]

Positive law must always be understood in its relation to the external "goods" and "requirements of practical reason" of which Finnis wrote. But, as Aquinas first saw, positive law is also a cultural artifact, something made by people for people. This quality of law as something constructed— i.e., made or done—by people supplies a distinctive normativity, separate and apart from the external ends for which law is created. Positive law has its own internal imperatives, in addition to external "goods" and "reasons." Some legal thinkers, most notably Lon Fuller, have labeled this normativity law's "inner morality."[3] This chapter is chiefly an exploration of law's purposes—the moral ends that are law's purpose—but it is worth emphasizing here that there are two moralities of law.

Lon Fuller spoke of "principles of legality": what law has to be like to be called "law" at all. Among these are requirements of publicity, promulgation, clarity, prospectivity, intelligibility, and, perhaps most important, congruence between the law as promulgated and the law as actually applied by state officials. Secret or indecipherable law fails as law: in such circumstances people are not able to order their actions according to law because they do not know what the law is. The last requirement stipulates that official action be governed by announced rules; arbitrary or capricious action is wrong. Some thinkers say that this last requirement inexorably leads to more just government, precisely by keeping official actions within promulgated standards. If the claim is true, we could say that law's inner morality necessarily promotes the moral goods that law is *for*, such as fair and equal treatment.[4]

Legal reasoning also has a peculiar internal logic. It is practical reasoning, or reasoning about what one ought to do. It is never a virtue of legal reasoning that it be sloppy or illogical. In addition to the virtues of ordinary reasoning, though, legal reasoning has some distinctive features: stipulated definitions, reasoning by analogy, and a heavy reliance on authority. These are the ingredients of what law professors call "thinking like a lawyer." Law schools teach this pretty well, too.

Because law has these internal benchmarks, one can evaluate it as *good* without implying that it is *just*.[5] "Bad law" might not be unjust at all; it might simply be confused or vague or erratic. "Bad law" might thus denote technical deficiency, and nothing more. Some legal scholars say that *Roe v. Wade* is "bad law," even while saying that they approve of abortion-on-demand. They mean, mostly, that the reasoning of the case is unconvincing.

Positive law so far considered is like any other human creation or performance. We say that Jane Austen was a good novelist and mean nothing about the kind of person she was. A great pitcher wins lots of games and has a low earned run average. But some great pitchers have been bad men. Pete Rose was a great hitter. He cannot get into the Hall of Fame, however, because he gambled on some baseball games. No one thinks that makes him less of a batter. Everyone understands that Rose suffers for misconduct "outside the lines," for character flaws and bad deeds that harmed the game's public reputation, for being a bad man and not a bad player. Bad baseball is just that: a poor performance according to the nonmoral evaluative criteria of the game.

Positive law can be judged—that is, evaluated as "good" or "bad"—on technical grounds, according to its "inner" morality, but it is the "outer" morality that counts most. The most important way to evaluate positive law is by its success or failure in contributing to the genuine flourishing of those persons it governs. That is what law is *for*. Those are the external ends for which law is called into being. These ends are real: they are not (like the law itself) artifacts or stipulations or legal fictions. The laws maintaining slavery, for example, were bad laws, no matter how clear and precise they were.

No doubt justice is one great end of law. Justice is concerned with giving to others their due. Positive law comes into being to shape life in political society. Neither justice nor law is involved straightforwardly in solely self-regarding acts (even though the number and kind of entirely self-regarding acts may be quite small). And so both justice and law naturally gravitate to questions of how we treat others.

I postpone until chapter 4 most of my explicit discussion of justice, where we take up the criminal *justice* system and its moral foundations. Until then this guide refers only occasionally to justice as the end of law for a simple reason: our law's greatest challenges are *prior* to justice: one needs to know to whom one owes duties of justice, in order to *do* justice. On this question our law and our law schools founder.

The positive law of political society is liable to the greatest injustice when it loses track of what law is *for*, that it is to serve not only persons but also the communities that help them to flourish. Justice depends not only upon correctly identifying those individuals to whom justice is due. It also has much to do with how the law treats human communities—marriage, family, religious organizations and so on. On these matters, too, our law and our law schools founder.

The greatest defect in our society's understanding of law is not that we have—speaking literally now—forgotten what law is for. We have not announced that henceforth human individuals exist to serve the greater good or the latest five-year plan. Americans are neither collectivists nor statists. We have not declared the *Volk* or the nation objects of veneration. Persons, marriage, family, and religion have been neither condemned nor ignored by our laws. Judges, legislators, and presidents all often speak most warmly of persons and their communities.

What has happened, and is happening, to our understanding of what law is for is subtler but no less portentous: we have come to mistakenly *define* what law is for. These mistakes do not result from unsuccessful efforts to get the matter right, unfortunately. Instead, lawmakers have lately deemed the truth about persons, marriage, family, and religion to be irrelevant to law. What these goods really are does not matter, they say. Worst of all, the irrelevance of moral truth has been carefully cultivated: *not* considering who is really a person, or what marriage really is, or how religion truly works, has been celebrated as a great virtue of American public life, a trend that has become dominant since World War II.

More exactly, under the influence of contemporary liberal doctrines about moral "neutrality," our determination of what law is *for* has become the creature of consensus, not of what *is*, of what is true.[6] The desideratum is not to get what law is *for* right, but to fit it all comfortably within dominant cultural mores and conventional morality. Our lawmakers have resolved that avoiding controversy is the overriding end of law, especially when it comes to considering what law is for. Our lawmakers correctly see that law's moral foundation is potentially a source of great controversy. What they fail to recognize is that getting it wrong promotes the greatest injustice of all.

Let us look, then, at how the law has recently identified and defined persons, the family rooted in marriage, and religion.

A. PERSONS

The Roman philosopher Justinian said that "[k]nowledge of law amounts to little if it overlooks the persons for whose sake law is made."[7] Justinian was right: persons are the basic realities for which law is called into existence. Law is for all persons, not for some persons for whose sake the law might subordinate other persons. It is a characteristic feature—an axiom, really—of modern legal regimes that positive law affects and applies to everyone equally, even to those who make the law. "Ours is a government of laws, not men," the famous saying holds. This is basically what "equality under law" means.

The most important provision in our fundamental law—the Constitution—is its guarantee to all "persons" of the "equal protection of the laws." All our legal rights and privileges depend on it. None of our rights and privileges would be secure if some people—those with the most money or power or those who complain the loudest—could arrange for other people not to count in law as "persons."

Slavery was one such arrangement. Slaveholders did not altogether deny that slaves were human persons. Slaveholders could see that slaves were reasoning beings, possessed of volition. Although many did not, there were also many slaveholders who recognized their slaves' humanity by according them religious instruction and respecting their family affairs. All slaveholders denied, though, that slaves enjoyed legal rights. A slave could never demand in court legal equality with his or her master. Slaves were persons whom the law treated for the sake of their masters. Slaves were their owners' property.

Most people need little help from the law to value their own well-being over the well-being of others, especially those not bound to them by blood or affinity. The allure of manipulating others is eminently understandable. One's life moves more easily when one can employ other persons as instruments for fulfilling one's own projects, ends, goals, and needs. Where the law fails to restrain such manipulation, where it sanctions subordination of some for the sake of others, great injustice results. In the wake of injustice comes rationalization, then later an ideology of inequality. Before long, a whole culture of subordination grows up, as feminists and pro-lifers and those who speak for African Americans have been right to remind us.

People do not need the law's help to exploit others. That comes naturally. They need the law's help to resist the temptation to manipulate. And, as a matter of historical fact, our constitutional guarantee of equality was enacted to deny the patina of legal sanction to slavery and all forms of peonage—to destroy them. The point of having "equal protection" is to forestall the arbitrary exercise of power by one set of persons over another. That seminal guarantee makes sense, though only if the question of who is a person refers to what is *true* in the case, and not to what we *want*. The force of equality is blunted if the stronger among us can declare the weaker to be "nonpersons," and then have their way with them. Again, legal equality is meaningless if the question of who counts as equal is itself resolved by strength, or wealth, or special pleading.

When we consider law's role in guaranteeing equal protection to all, regardless of privilege or dominance, we can see how our permissive abortion laws strike at the moral foundations of law. The premise on which opposition to permissive abortion laws is based is that they involve injustice towards a class of human beings—the unborn. The content of abortion laws is the main thing, not how they came to be. That is to say, if the law of abortion, or of any other important matter, were resolved by a coin flip, or through trial by ordeal, or by which side could make the most jump shots in a row—and resolved correctly—the law would be just. However, those who decided by making legal decisions so arbitrarily would have acted unjustly nonetheless, for they would have played with others' lives, leaving to a contest of irrelevant skills a crucial moral decision. For anyone trying to understand how law is related to moral truth, the jump-shooters' example would be an amazing case study of what not to do.

In the same way, what has happened recently with persons and their communities is a remarkable case study of what not to do. There has been a fundamental shift from considering the law as established to protect all persons to a view that law has the power to define what a person *is*. If it can define personhood, law has the power to grant privileges but also to withhold them, depending on how personhood is defined. Using this method, protection becomes a matter of arbitrary legal definition, as arbitrary as a legal decision made by taking jump shots, rather than an inherently guaranteed right. The consequences of allowing lawyers and justices to define personhood, those whose rights will be guaranteed under the law, are illustrated in the following example.

A New York court decision, the *Byrn* case, was the precursor to *Roe v. Wade*. It held that "[w]hat is a legal person is for the law . . . to *say*, which simply means that upon *according* legal personality to a thing the law affords it the rights and privileges of a legal person." (emphasis added).[8] The court was poised to treat the "person" question as a prerogative of the law, as if the law—more exactly, the *Byrn* court positioned to make the law—might grant a privilege that, as the court made clear, could also be withheld. The *Byrn* court rejected, in other words, the possibility that, because of the kind of beings they were, unborn children have rights that even courts are bound to respect.

In an arresting passage, the *Byrn* court wrote that "the process" of deciding who is a person "is circular because it is definitional." The judges thought that identifying what law is for was a dead end, so long as law's ends were thought to be external to the law itself. Of course they are. But the court declared that the proper (noncircular) way to view the question is as a "policy determination whether legal personality should attach and not a question of biological or 'natural' correspondence."[9]

Roe v. Wade took the same path. Writing for the Supreme Court of the United States in that case, Justice Harry Blackmun conceded that if the unborn were recognized in law as persons there could be no right to abortion. Abortion would then be constitutionally prohibited homicide. To avoid that conclusion—and it is impossible to understand *Roe* without presuming that the court wanted to avoid that conclusion—Blackmun said that he would put aside the question of whether unborn human individuals were, in reality, human persons. He declared that the court did not "need to resolve the difficult question of when life begins."[10] The court inquired into matters of limited, technical usage: are the unborn "legal" or "constitutional" persons in the "whole sense"? As in the *Byrn* case, the question of who counts was turned in upon itself, made into a "policy" question about what we *want* to do. Again, there is no suggestion that our hands are tied by the inherent dignity of the unborn.

Blackmun resolved the question of whom the law of homicide was *for* entirely within the boundaries of positive law. He was wrong even about that; positive law had for centuries treated abortion as homicide, and prohibited it for that reason. But the wrong answer to the wrong question—however remarkable and consequential it is—is not our concern here. Our concern is that he never looked outside the law at all to consider an underlying moral reality, as he did when it came to the woman's asserted right to abortion. Abortion had been legally prohibited from time out of mind. There was no chance that looking within the law for a right to abortion would yield the desired answer. For that reason, Blackmun catalogued at length the sources of a woman's possible distress at an unwanted pregnancy. This "distress" was no legal fiction. He referred entirely to real-world difficulties, never to what constituted "legal" or "constitutional" distress in the "whole" sense. Had Blackmun looked at the conventional legal sources on which he relied to dispose of "personhood," he would have discovered that the law never deemed the distress of pregnancy—however real—a justification or an excuse for an abortion. There can be little doubt that the unborn were finally considered not to be "persons" in *Roe* because the needs of others—Blackmun's "distressed" women—dictated that they could not be.

Academic apologists for *Roe* have sought to buttress the court's decisive move, its choice to treat "person" as a restricted matter of legal reasoning, as a policy-driven sojourn into a fictional realm. Ronald Dworkin is among the top five legal philosophers of the last generation. He defends *Roe* for treating "person" as if it were a synonym for "member." Dworkin would include within the law's protection only those candidates whose applications are ratified by those who consider themselves already initiated. Whether someone is to be counted a person would depend upon the choices of others. For Dworkin, the key is acceptance: legal protection against arbitrary violence extends to those who are admitted to society's membership according to "genetic or geographical or other historical conditions identified by *social practice*" (emphasis added).[11] Like Blackmun and the rest of the *Roe* court, Dworkin does not regard the constitutional question about persons as transparent for the truth of the matter.

John Rawls is considered to be the English-speaking world's preeminent political theorist since World War II. His master work, *A Theory of Justice*, has organized political theory as an academic discipline since its publication in 1970. Rawls follows, and then trumps, Dworkin and Blackmun in defending abortion rights. Like Blackmun and Dworkin, Rawls declines to ask whether residents of the womb are, in truth, persons. He goes beyond Blackmun and Dworkin by saying that any investigation into the truth would be *unjust*. The question is forbidden; asking it would violate the norms of respectful public discourse that he calls "public reason."

Rawls's reasoning, in an argument that has become famous, is that recourse in public deliberation to "comprehensive doctrines" could cause bitter social strife. And he contends that asking who is really a person would invoke a banned "comprehensive doctrine." What is the alternative? How *could* people in society ascertain *who* law is *for*, save by exchanging views about what is the case: who really *is* a person? Rawls sets up the question addressed in *Roe* as a "balance" of three values: orderly reproduction of political society over time; women's equality; and, finally, "respect for human life."[12] Rawls himself concludes (in his 1993 book *Political Liberalism*) that only "a reasonable balance" of these values is a fit way for our democracy to resolve the abortion issue—and that "any" reasonable balance gives women a right to choose abortion.

Why did the court in *Roe* do what it did? After all, it could not follow Dworkin and Rawls, who wrote post hoc. *Byrn* was a precedent from an inferior court, and nothing in the Supreme Court's own precedents came close—by Blackmun's own admission—to justifying abortion rights. What was going on? The biographer of Justice Lewis Powell, who voted with Blackmun, reports that the idea that a "fertilized embryo was a fully recognized human life would always seem to him unacceptably remote from ordinary experience."[13] This notion of "experience" as law's ground resonates with the court's privileging of women's psychological and financial "distress" over the "difficult theological and philosophical" question of when life begins.[14] Justice William Brennan, who also voted with the *Roe* majority, wrote in an internal memo that "the law deals in reality, not obscurity . . . [or] speculation"—in obvious reference to retreating from the question of who or what law is *for*.[15] At least for Powell, the fact that the belief in the personhood of unborn children "was closely associated with the Catholic Church only made it easier to dismiss."[16] The *Roe* court did not give a reasoned answer to the personhood question, choosing silently to ignore it. This glaring defect, Powell thought, would be forgiven eventually by popular "satisfaction with the result." History would vindicate *Roe*. And so *Roe* turned on what people supposedly wanted, not on the question of a person's intrinsic worth and inherent dignity—with the added twist that the justices went over the heads of their contemporaries and appealed to tomorrow's wants.[17]

What happened in *Roe* to persons has since happened to the communities that contribute most to persons' genuine flourishing: marriage, and the family rooted in marriage, and religious societies, including churches. They, too, have been fictionalized by our law to serve other "policies." These "policies" are bound up with the interests of the stronger, the "elites," and with the desire of these elites to sever law from objective moral norms.

B. Marriage

The most prominent example of our law's recent treatment of marriage came in a Hawaii Supreme Court case, the first in a line of judicial decisions favoring marriage for same-sex couples. The precise result of *Baehr v. Lewin* is not our present concern. Our interest is in how the judges conceived of the relationship between moral truth about marriage and the law of marriage.

In *Baehr,* Hawaii defended its marriage laws by saying that they—the laws limiting marriage to one man and one woman—were in line with what marriage really is. The state's attorney general argued that "[m]arriage was a custom long before the state commenced to issue licenses" for it. He added that marriage "has always been considered as a union of a man and a woman." The attorney general pointed out that, because of what marriage *is,* the law did not discriminate against the same-sex couples in the case who sought to be married. Their relationship does not "authorize the issuance of a marriage license because what they propose *is not a marriage*" (emphasis added).[18]

The court brusquely rejected this whole argument as "an exercise in tortured and conclusory sophistry." The state's effort to illumine legal marriage by reference to the moral reality was "tautological," "circular and unpersuasive."[19] Like the *Byrn* court when it considered who was a person, the Hawaii court thought that any reference to the moral reality of marriage evaded the question of what the law of marriage should be. This position that there should be an opaque barrier between law and truth regarding marriage has found its way to the United States Supreme Court, too. Justice Brennan observed in one case that "[e]ven if we can agree . . . that 'family' and 'parenthood' are part of the good life, it is absurd to assume that we can agree on the content of those terms and destructive to pretend that we do."[20] The Supreme Court has not yet ruled on same-sex marriage. When it does, it is more likely than not to follow Brennan's—and Hawaii's—lead in severing what law is for from the truth about the most important human community: marriage.[21]

People seeking the truth about marriage have often gone wrong. Inquiry into the truth of any matter—even important matters such as personhood and marriage—is no guarantee of success. Even if the law's mistakes about marriage are blameless errors, because of these errors people will not flourish as they should.

Why? How are people's opportunities for genuine flourishing affected by matters so mundane as the law's definition of marriage? After all, the law does not "impose" its definition on anyone. Does it really matter so much what the law says, or does not say, about marriage?

It does. When it comes to law and marriage (and much else, for that matter), the law really does have a trickle-down effect. The "marriage" available in any society is powerfully formed by law and by the culture, which is itself powerfully shaped by law.[22] As Oxford legal philosopher Joseph Raz has written, "monogamy, assuming that it is the only valuable form of marriage, cannot be practiced by an individual. It requires a culture which recognizes it, and which supports it through the public's attitude and through its formal institutions."[23] Corrupt culture and law conspire to deprive people of the opportunity to choose (real) marriage where, for example, polygamy is the social norm, or where wives are treated as chattel. In the latter situation, where true equality and mutuality between spouses is unimaginable because of false beliefs about the inferior nature of women, marriage as a two-in-one-flesh communion is simply not available as a choice.

Now, Raz does not suppose that, in a culture whose law and public morality do not support monogamy, someone who happens to believe in it will be unable to restrict himself to having one wife or will be required to take additional wives. The point, as expressed by Princeton's Robert George, is rather that

> even if monogamy is a key element of a sound understanding of marriage, large numbers of people will fail to understand that or why that is the case—and will therefore fail to grasp the value of monogamy and the intelligible point of practicing it—unless they are assisted by a culture which supports monogamous marriage. Marriage is the type of good which can be participated in, or fully participated in, only by people who properly understand it and choose it with a proper understanding in mind; yet people's ability properly to understand it, and thus to choose it, depends upon institutions and cultural understandings that transcend individual choice.[24]

C. Religion

The state could compel persons to attend religious services. Compelling people to show up somewhere at a specific time is commonplace, as compulsory school laws, jury duty, subpoenaed witnesses, and conscription all make clear. But subpoenaing worshipers is a very bad idea. Compelling people to patronize churches would do them little good as a religious exercise. People answering a legal summons would scarcely be professing free assent to proposed truths of faith, voluntarily giving homage to God, or willingly joining in a communal ritual. Compelling people to attend church would make them be present and that is all. In rare circumstances, even that might do them some good—by sheltering them from harm during a military attack, for instance. But it would not make them more religious, any more than doing the dishes would make husbands good if the state made it a misdemeanor for husbands to refuse to do so: husbands would be doing the right thing for the wrong reason, i.e., in order to stay out of jail.

When it comes to law, religion is like marriage in three important ways: neither is a creature of the law; both need some help from the law to flourish; each is the type of activity or association whose value depends on freedom in important ways. People have to embrace religion and marriage freely to participate in them properly, and to realize the moral benefits that each offers. (That was Professor George's point about marriage.) So we prize religious liberty and look to the law to promote our free embrace of faith.

Religious liberty is not always convenient for the state. History is full of stories of political rulers who tried to take over, corrupt, pacify, and otherwise domesticate the spiritual loyalties of a people. Many succeeded. Americans wondered during World War II why Jehovah's Witnesses should be treated by the law exactly as other believers were treated. Jehovah's Witnesses denied allegiance to all earthly forms of government, refused to salute the flag for which men and women were dying every day, and habitually—and raucously—denounced Roman Catholics at nearly every opportunity. Perhaps there is always one religious group or another that especially rankles and therefore causes many to ask, why do we protect religious liberty to the extent that we do?

There are many possible answers to the question of why public authority would accord people freedom of religion. There is no doubt that the whole tradition of religious liberty in America, however, is rooted in the idea of the truth of religion. I do not mean that our law has surveyed all the different churches' liturgies, doctrines, and creeds, and said, "Here is the one true way. There is no other!" Not at all. Our legal tradition is rooted in convictions about what God really wants from people, and about what counts as genuine religious observance and faith. Our tradition is founded in convictions such as those expressed by James Madison, our fourth president and a moving force behind our Bill of Rights. Madison wrote that religion involved duties to a creator God that God wished men to perform because it is right to perform them, not because of fear of legal sanction.[25]

In the next chapter we shall investigate further the relationship between religion, morality, and our constitutional order, but for present purposes two observations about our law's recent treatment of religion are in order. One is that for the last forty years the main story line in church-state law has been the ascendancy of political convenience over religious freedom: in constitutional language, "nonestablishment" has subordinated "free exercise." This story line means that fears of religion's ill effects on society—divisiveness, intolerance, and authoritarianism—have justified deep incursions into religious freedom. Such incursions have included wiping out all directed religious expression in public schools, removal of religious symbols from public space, and unremitting hostility to public aid to religious education (hostility only somewhat lessened recently by the emergence of vouchers in a few cities and states). All the ill effects of religion cited to justify these incursions have been prophesied much more than they have been proven. More importantly, even a surface reading of church-state law's main story line calls into question whether or not lawmakers have considered the idea that law is for persons and their communities, including their religious communities, and not the other way around.

The second observation cuts still deeper, and is closer to the theme of this chapter on law's corroded moral foundations. Religion in the law's eyes looks quite different than it does in the eyes of most Americans. Any dictionary will tell you that religion has to do with a greater than human source of meaning and value, which most people refer to as "God." Religion so understood is not the same thing as a personal philosophy, a human convention, or the like. But where the free exercise of religion is concerned, courts have subsumed human beings' beliefs about a transcendent source of meaning and placed them under a wider individual autonomy untethered to faith. "Religion" is just one aspect of a broader freedom of choice whose ground is not God or what God expects of persons; it is personal authenticity.

The crowning moment of the main story line on church-state law occurred in *Planned Parenthood v. Casey*, a 1992 Supreme Court decision that affirmed *Roe v. Wade*. The court in *Casey* tied together several threads of cases having to do with legal treatment of marriage, family, and sexual morality. Why, the court asked, does our law "afford protection to personal decisions relating to marriage, procreation, contraception [and] family relationships?" Not because of any moral truth about marriage, family, or religion. The court said instead that the common underlying value is personal authenticity. These choices are "central to personal dignity and autonomy." "At the heart of liberty," the court concluded, "is the right to define one's own concept of existence, of meaning, of the universe, and of the mystery of human life."[26] In other words, "at the heart of liberty" is moral subjectivism, not objective moral truth. The ability to determine what constitutes the mystery of human life with reference only to the self is called the *Casey* "Mystery Passage."

Religion properly understood has to do with the transcendent, the supernatural, "the substance of things hoped for, the evidence of things unseen."[27] Religion so understood is a barrier to the human tendency to make human beings—instead of God—the source of meaning and value. The above "Mystery Passage" reverses this traditional understanding by making the individual will into the source or criterion of value when it comes to matters of the most significance. This is a reason why one should be ambivalent about religious liberty in our law: religious liberty has to do fundamentally with persons as the source of meaning and value for themselves.

The more serious underlying danger is the collapse of moral objectivity itself. The ground of—"heart of"—liberty is now defined as choosing, a ground selected by the court for two reasons. One reason is that choice is more or less equally distributed: all persons have at least the capacity, if not the present actual ability, to think and choose. The second reason is that choosing is central to dignity and autonomy. Choosing makes me into the person I really am. The combined effect of the two grounds is to make my beliefs and conduct worthy of full respect, not because they are true, but only because they are really mine. Because they are central to who I am, criticizing my beliefs or conduct demeans and injures me. Equal respect for me entails, at least in law, that my concept of life be treated as equally true (or valued or sound) as yours—and everyone else's. And so the great guarantee of legal equality joins "the heart of liberty" in thrall to moral subjectivism.

D. Moral Foundations of Law

This strange inversion of value leads straightway to what I call the "transparency" problem in public discourse. Sometimes when we say that pornography or the recreational use of narcotics or sodomy or abortion is wrong, we say that it is "my" view or part of "my moral code." This way of speaking can be an innocent locution for the proposition "pornography is simply wrong." It can be misleading, however, when used in our culture and law, given their moral subjectivism. In that case, when one says that pornography is wrong, one is heard to say that it is "my" morality that makes it wrong. The judgment then is now a fact about me. "Your" morality might see it quite differently. Then where do we go?

Judges have run wild with this "transparency" problem in erasing laws meant to protect public morals. The "transparency" problem as it appears in judicial opinions relies upon one judgment, perceived to be correct in the interest of furthering the desired line of argument: the fact that a judgment is mine is not a reason for the state to act in a certain way. That one declares oneself opposed to pornography or promiscuity or recreational drug use is, in truth, no reason for restrictive public policies on pornography. It is not a reason at all. It is just a fact. In our culture, the fact is most likely to be understood as a report about one's feelings or emotions, as if one were saying, "I find dirty magazines repugnant." But feelings are not reasons either, no matter how strong they are.

The trick in this judicial gambit is this: no one really thinks that the fact of holding a view is a reason for action, unless the underlying reasons for why one holds the view to be true are considered. Almost no one says, "I am opposing this practice because it is my view that I am opposing this practice." People say instead, "I am opposed because it is wrong in the following way. . . . That's my view."

Most people who say that homosexual activity, for example, is wrong mean that it is wrong for everyone, that it is objectively and categorically immoral. This view could be false. If it is, its falsity is sufficient reason to discard the judgment and everything it might entail. Saying that a negative judgment about homosexual behavior is "just your view and it would be unfair to impose your view upon someone who does not share it would be wrong" evades the matter asserted: homosexual acts are wrong *simpliciter*, for you and me and everybody. Saying "it's just your view" is also self-refuting, for the judgment that imposing one's view on others is "wrong" is, one could just as well say, merely your view of justice—and it would be wrong for you to impose your view on me.

In contrast to the opaque or intransitive quality of moral judgment evidenced above, judicial conclusions in favor of permissive laws—for pornography, assisted suicide, same-sex marriage, and the like—are offered as transparent with reference to why the view is held. When courts refer to their favored moral conclusion they do not brand it as merely their view, based on judicial feelings. When courts offer their favored conclusion they assert that the matter of justice is so. Full stop. There is no mention of anyone's possessory interest in justice, save when it comes to arguments against the court's conclusions. Convictions offered in opposition to the court's arguments are often dismissed as raw majoritarian preferences.

The United States Supreme Court habitually ducks critical questions by playing the transparency card. Consider the case of *Lawrence v. Texas*. From the founding of our country in 1789 until *Lawrence* came down in 2003, public authority was free to declare that sexual conduct outside of marriage was wrong, and could even be made criminal. As Justice John Harlan wrote approvingly in the 1961 case of *Poe v. Ullman*, laws regarding marriage are meant to "provide both when the sexual powers may be used and the legal and societal context in which children are born and brought up, as well as laws forbidding adultery, fornication and homosexual practices, which express the negative of the proposition. . . ."[28]

Lawrence v. Texas was a case involving claims of two homosexual men caught in the act. The Supreme Court concluded that it would be wrong—"demeaning," unfairly discriminatory, arbitrary—to treat the sexual desires of homosexuals any differently than those of heterosexuals, including heterosexuals who are married to each other. The leading effect of *Lawrence* was to overturn the tradition articulated by Justice Harlan: *Lawrence* made consent and privacy, not marriage, the legally enforceable moral principles of sexual conduct. *Lawrence's* reasoning underlies the widespread concern that this case will provide precedent for the eventual constitutional recognition of same-sex marriages. A majority of the United States Supreme Court really did say that homosexuals have as much interest in constitutional protection for their choices concerning marriage, family, contraception, and procreation as do heterosexual persons.[29]

The *Lawrence* ruling strategically depended upon the transparency problem and the *Casey* "Mystery Passage." The majority opinion by Justice Kennedy spoke of society's "animosity toward the class of persons affected" as one reason for the *Lawrence* decision (relying on another case involving alleged discrimination against homosexuals, *Romer v. Evans*).[30] Justice O'Connor said in her separate opinion that "moral disapproval of this group [i.e., homosexuals], like a bare desire to harm the group" has no standing in our constitutional order. Of course not: a reported feeling, or a statement of hostility, or the fact that many people believe sodomy to be immoral does not make sodomy immoral. None of these is a good reason for state policy because none is a reason at all. Justice O'Connor thus correctly concluded that "moral disapproval," in the sense of "a bare desire to harm" others, is not a legitimate state interest.[31]

But Justice O'Connor and the majority begged the real question, an evasion aided and abetted by their use of the transparency problem. If we do not assume as they did that "moral disapproval" is an unreasoned prejudice, then we would have to confront an additional question, a question which the court chose not to face: Is it true that homosexual acts are wrong? If it is true that they are wrong, then homosexual acts are harmful to the persons who perform them. If these acts are harmful to those who perform them, legal discouragement can help them to avoid immoral acts. Legal discouragement can help them to improve their character. Having laws or policies in place that instantiate the proposition that sodomy is wrong can also help all of us. Such laws would then form part of our society's moral ecology, and thus reinforce persons' belief that sodomy is wrong. This reinforcement would educate the young, especially, about the right path to take when it comes to sexual activity.

The *Lawrence* court pronounced instead that laws which imply that homosexual acts are wrong are acts of gross injustice to homosexuals. That "injustice" was, the court asserted, objective and unqualified; it was not a report of the justices' feelings or a fact about them. They said, quoting from *Casey*: "Our obligation is to define the liberty of all, not to mandate our own moral code."[32] Maybe so: the justices' "own" morality is no ground of law, or of anything at all. It is just a fact about them. What they mean, however, is something quite different, and much more momentous. They mean that no one's idea of morality (including theirs) supplies the ground of liberty in our constitutional order. And that leaves no objective morality at all: even moral truth has to be articulated by someone.

2. LAW, CULTURE, MORALITY— AND RELATIVISM

YOU ARE DRIVING HOME for a holiday dinner. The weather is clear, the road is well paved, and traffic is light. The posted speed limit is sixty miles per hour. In light of the good conditions and the quality of your car, you judge that you could do about seventy-five without any danger to others or to yourself. You wonder, "should I obey the speed limit anyway?"

Through this window into your thoughts, we see that you believe there is no moral truth that requires drivers to go sixty mph, and no more. You figure that the relevant objective moral norm is more general, something like "drive safely, in light of all the relevant conditions." The posted speed limit is somebody's idea—state legislators, probably— of what is generally safe. Your question, though, is particular to here and now. You think that safety is not the only issue. If it were, the law would simply forbid driving; that way, nobody would get hurt. But almost nobody would get to where they wanted to go, either. The posted speed limit represents, you conclude, a balance of safety and efficiency. Other balances might be just as defensible. You conclude that sixty mph is a legislative choice of one reasonable option from among several. You are tempted to conclude from that line of reasoning that you are free to make a reasonable choice of your own to go seventy-five. You are ready to say *Avanti!*

Your conclusion about the speed limit is sound: it could reasonably be different. The speed limit is part of the *positive* law—the law handed down ("posited") by human authority. It is not a divine directive, even though sometimes—if not this time—the law mimics a moral truth: for example, the crime of perjury is little more than "do not bear false witness against your neighbor." But most often the law represents an authoritative choice from among two or more proposals, each one an apt way to put into practice some general moral requirement, such as using the road in a way that does not endanger others or yourself. Options not chosen are not therefore unreasonable. They just were not chosen. They are not the law.

It has famously been said that if men were angels no government would be necessary. That is not true. In a society of angels no sanctions or punishment would be needed; we could count on goodwill and everyone's desire to do what is workable. But with almost all coordination problems—including those involving beings of goodwill—more than one scheme is right. Often, many are. Even a company of angels could not know what is "right" in, say, the Battle of Armageddon, without an authoritative choice of one plan of attack. Reflection upon life in human society tells us that broad moral norms, such as fairness, are the basic drives that make decent common life possible. But some authoritative means of making that drive specific is necessary to effective cooperation, on the road and all across the board. Just think of what it would be like if drivers could choose the left or the right side of the road as each one fancied.

Law is not a command, but it performs that function in solving the coordination problems endemic to any common plan, activity, or project. Some publicly recognized, concrete plan or structure is essential to social life. Having a common plan is thus morally necessary, although no one plan in particular is required by morality. Only choice can settle the matter.[33]

In the example above, although your reasoning is sound, your conclusion is wrong. You think that if seventy-five is just as reasonable as sixty—and it may be—then it would be reasonable (i.e., right) for you to choose to go seventy-five even though the law is sixty. But this conclusion ignores the most important thing one needs to know about positive law, which is that legal norms are not *suggestions* about what you might want to consider doing. Law is prescriptive in a much stronger sense than that. It is a *reason* for action for those whose law it is. Legal norms are very special, powerful reasons: law displaces one's own unfettered deliberations about what to do, even if one's deliberations are entirely reasonable. Law is a jealous master of conscience: at least presumptively, one is morally obliged to adhere to the law.

It is this quality of law which you—as driver—have been facing. Legal norms are "exclusionary" reasons. The law's "most elementary claim on my attention [is] its claim to direct certain choices of mine, [and] to override my self-interest in certain respects."[34] Legal norms override more than self-interest, for the individual judgments law displaces do not necessarily involve ego. The law's unique contribution to social order is its claim to clearly and certainly light the way by which we may cooperate. It does so precisely by marking out the *one* path of social cooperation. Once the law has been settled, continued pursuit of one's own ideas about cooperation would undermine this contribution.

Law's distinctive contribution to social order works in ways great and small. A small way is speed limits on the highway. A great way would be the state's decision to build the highway. Building the whole interstate system was itself a choice, made back in the 1950s by responsible officials of the United States government. The choice could have been different; in fact, many modern societies have chosen to rely much more than ours has on public (chiefly rail) transportation between cities. America's decision to build roads instead of trains has had immense, lasting significance for our nation—just as have other choices from among reasonable options concerning farm policy, homeowners' benefits, foreign relations, etc.

All these choices have shaped the United States into the nation it is. Each of these decisions could have been different; if any had been different, we would be different. And, even if we, or our parents or grandparents, fought hard for alternatives not chosen back in the fifties, we, and they, are morally obliged to cooperate according to law once the fateful decisions have been reached. It was legitimate to argue against building interstates, and against the implicit corollary commitment we made to build a nation around the internal combustion engine. Anyone who honestly believed that interstates and all they implied would do more harm than good was probably duty-bound to argue against them. When we think about what the need for oil has meant for our politics, we might think that those opposed to the interstate might even have been right. But it would have been wrong for them to refuse to pay their fair share of taxes for highway construction, or to break the rules of the road in protest, once the matter was decided. Building highways rather than railways was not unjust or unconscionable. Cooperating with that decision would not have involved us, or our parents or grandparents, in performing immoral acts. Once it was the highway and not the railway, then, cooperation was morally required.

But back to our highway driving example. Soaring thoughts about the law's unique powers do not impress you. You are still behind the steering wheel, checking your watch every five minutes. Another way of looking at the speed limit now comes to your mind, brought into focus by the preceding comments about law as choice. A different legislative choice—sixty-five, seventy, or seventy-five mph—would have been just as reasonable as the choice your state's legislators actually made. You think that a higher limit would be more reasonable than that which you see on the passing road signs. Some neighboring states agree: they have sixty-five and seventy mph speed limits. In the mountain states, some have limits of seventy-five mph. In Germany, amazingly, they have no highway speed limit at all.

You tell yourself the speed limit in your state is arbitrary. It is just some powerful group's say-so about things. Maybe, you begin to rationalize, some legislators have a financial stake in the choice of sixty mph; others have been bamboozled by "greens" who say slower traffic is better for the environment. You conclude by saying to yourself, "I am not obliged to go along. I may have to comply grudgingly with the speed limit, but only because I can't afford another ticket. There is nothing morally obligatory about adopting the law as a reason for my actions. I'll do what I please, and pay the darn speeding ticket."

This way of looking at the situation is accurate, too—up to a limited point. One can look at the law as a *fact*, as a sheer given. Other people made the law without asking your advice. Maybe you never voted to put any of them in charge. Maybe, even, the law is unwise. But there it is, all the same, staring you in the face, beyond your control now as much as today's weather.

The temptation you, our driver, are experiencing is to go beyond a limited recognition of law as fact. You imagine law as an unwelcome intrusion, as an unreasonable impediment to what you really want to do. After all, law claims priority over self-interest; law does not purport to unerringly harmonize with your desires, needs, and goals. You are tempted to view the speed limit as merely a conditional threat: if you speed and get stopped, you will have to pay a fine. That's all. Whether you choose to speed, then, becomes a comparison between your desire to get home and that fine, discounted by the likelihood that you will be stopped.

Oliver Wendell Holmes dubbed this viewpoint the "bad man's" way of looking at law. In a famous speech in 1897 Holmes declared, "The prophecies of what the courts will do in fact, and nothing more pretentious, are what I mean by the law."[35] The "bad" man does not treat legal norms as reasons for action. He treats them instead as indications of what will happen to him if he chooses a path outside the law. What matters to his decision is the probable consequence of acting contrary to the law.

Holmes's "bad man" is the progenitor of contemporary legal realism. "Legal realists" characteristically deny that legal norms constitute the real reasons for people's actions, including especially the actions of those who wield judicial authority. In the case of "realist" judges, the court's opinion would be a rhetorical display for public consumption, an ideological construct, or some kind of required written excuse for a decision reached—per realist hypotheses—on other grounds, usually self-interested class or economic motives. When it comes to the ordinary driver, realists follow Holmes's "bad man": the law and consequences of violating it are data important for deciding what to do. But that's it, nothing more. There is no moral obligation to make the law the reason for my choices.

Holmes's "bad man" is not entirely a fictional character. All of us sometimes see law as Holmes said we should habitually see it, or perhaps we often slip into his more jaded point of view. But Holmes did not offer up the "bad man" as an occasional pose. He offered it as a normative construct, a perspective in which to make sense of law as such, not just a rationalizer's device for occasional misbehavior. The "bad man" does not just beckon us to speed on down the highway. He calls for a much larger commitment than that.

But Holmes was wrong: law cannot consistently and coherently be seen as the "bad man" sees it. Even if we decide to speed on the interstate, we had better not speed in the classroom. We may occasionally choose as Holmesian "bad men" do and step on the gas (*Avanti!*). But we will never understand law if we make our occasional choices into an intellectual paradigm. If we do, we will miss much that is important about law as a uniquely valuable way to order social life.

The limited plausibility of Holmes's "bad man" and the temptation to be "bad men" on the road sets up an alluring trap for the law student. There is no denying that law has a double life. Law is both prescriptive ("ought") and descriptive ("is"). Law can be viewed internally, from the perspective of the deliberating and choosing person who seeks to freely cooperate with others. Viewed this way, legal norms all but settle my choice to drive sixty mph. I might do so even if there were no consequences.

Law can also be viewed externally, as a simple fact about what others have said. We speak all the time about the laws of other countries or of certain religions, the laws of physics and of nature. But none of these laws enters into our conscientious deliberation. None claims the prerogative to direct our choices.

The common danger to law students is not the whole-hearted adoption of the "bad man's" perspective. Rather, it is oscillating between the internal and external points of view. We might treat law as an outside intrusion and consider only the costs of noncompliance when it is to our advantage to do so. When others break the law, however, especially to our disadvantage, we might slip back into a moralistic vision of legal norms as binding: how dare he or she cut me off in traffic! In the classroom we might adopt the internal point of view when we like the results: race discrimination is wrong, really and truly wrong, and that's why the law prohibits it. But when it comes to certain moral laws, perhaps, we flip to the external point of view: laws prohibiting extramarital sex are relics of the past; that they were enacted and reenacted for centuries is just a fact about generations long gone. Anyone who today argues for retaining them is just trying to impose his morality on others who do not share it.

This type of oscillation can be simply (but not merely!) a moral problem. It can be just a temptation to opportunism, to dealing with others unfairly. We are concerned here with another kind of problem, however, a problem of understanding and not of will. Oscillating, or flipping, between the internal and the external viewpoints is a sure route to misunderstanding the law and the relationships among people whose law it is. Oscillating between viewpoints is to invite variable matters of fact—of description—to take charge of the task of moral judgment. After all, facts about people—individuals, small communities, even large societies—vary at any given moment in world history. Individuals and groups also change their minds over time. The *Casey* "Mystery Passage" slipped subjectivism into law's moral foundation, with ill effects all around. Flipping from the "good" to "bad" man's way of looking at law introduces moral relativism. And that will not do very well, either.

The challenge is to retain the internal view of law without denying what is true about the external perspective of law. Can we integrate the "ought" and "is" of law in one stable story about law?

Yes, we can. In fact, we have already done so: our whole first chapter described how positive law is a huge cultural artifact—a product (if you will) made for people and presented to the community as a given. But we saw, too, that this edifice is dedicated to serving real moral ends: what law is for, its purpose. All we need to do now is extend and refine the point of chapter 1.

John Finnis writes that "for the sake of justice and a flourishing community of people in good [moral] shape . . . we need the set of rules, arrangements, processes, institutions and persons with responsibility and thus authority, the set [we commonly call the] law." That "law"—say, the law of Indiana or of the United Kingdom—is a vast cultural artifact posited by people to order their common life. For the sake of justice we need these rules to be "clear, general, stable, capable of being complied with and explicable to any fair-minded person."[36] To put the point differently still: law works only where it achieves the appearance of solidity, as if it were a nonnegotiable fact of social interaction. Additionally, law only works where people voluntarily accept it and internalize it.

Legal authority is thus a kind of moral authority. Legal reasoning is a kind of moral reasoning. Legal norms are good (that is, moral) reasons for acting—all because law is part of the answer to the question, What, all things considered, is the right thing for me to do? Law contributes to resolving that question by offering direction which, presumptively or prima facie, we are morally obliged to accept. This presumption of law's moral bindingness can be defeated, however, and is overcome in instances where the law would direct me to do what morality holds I must never do. Thus, there can be morally justified lawbreaking.[37]

So then, what if most people speed? What if many who do not speed refrain for emotional reasons, and do not refrain from speeding because they think speeding is wrong? What if, in other words, most people think speeding is OK? What if most people, when it comes to speeding (or for that matter, parking rules, business regulations, or even income-tax issues), are legal realists: the "law" means do what you wish and accept the price if you are caught?

With these questions, something different has entered the picture. We have seen that civil law is normative: law aims to guide deliberation by supplying reasons for action. Critically justified morality does that as well. We have seen, too, how these two prescriptive sources can be integrated. Morality justifies lawmakers' authority as a particularly effective way to guide and secure cooperation in political society for the common good. It is reasonable to accept this guidance as an "exclusionary reason." Now the "morality" offered in a society—call it "conventional morality"—appears as a competing indicator of what you should decide to do.

But we are not yet done with complications. For example, let us say that most people you know think that speeding is "cool." They say that driving within the posted limit is for rule-followers and mama's boys. It is widely supposed, moreover, that police officers tolerate driving up to ten miles over the speed limit. There is a permissive culture of the road, a culture which is out of sync with the posted speed limit.

In this case, the civil law's directiveness is blunted, not by a contrary norm of conventional morality, but by the larger web of meanings and images we call culture. Stated more exactly, conventional morality, being a part of culture, takes on added force when its directiveness is gilded by cultural embellishments, especially those which engage our vanity and insecurity. (Think of how most advertising combines useful information about a consumer product's genuine benefits with seductive emotional and psychological appeals.) We saw before that to understand law is to understand it as really directive, as entering into deliberation and choice. We saw that law is a cultural product as well. We saw, too, how one can regard the positive law of one's own country as a kind of legal anthropology, simply as information about what the powerful have said. In fact, this is pretty much *all* that law amounted to, according to Oliver Wendell Holmes and his many followers among judges and law professors today. (For more on legal theories as prescriptive and descriptive, see appendix E.)

Now we see that culture and convention can be rival sources of directiveness. Understanding law requires that we consider it as competing with cultural and conventional signals concerning what I truly should decide. That is our aspiring speeder's question: "What should I truly decide to do, in light of law, conventional morality, and cultural values?"

Trying to understand law is now starting to look a bit like flying an airplane. Flying mishaps are not inevitable. Misunderstanding law is not inevitable, either. But each task is unforgiving of small mistakes. Flip a plane and it is a long way down. Flip into subjectivism or relativism when studying law and the ground slips right out from beneath you. Staying on the right track requires, in both cases, constant vigilance and effort. No exhaustive set of instructions is possible. There is no set of written directions to avoid error forevermore. No inoculation is available. No huge, three-dimensional diagram of all the moving parts in proper alignment is available. Learning to understand law is not learning how to use a gadget. But a number of illustrations will help, and may suffice to educate the student enough so that he or she can fly solo the rest of the way.

Culture includes the matters that archaeologists and other anthropologists study: pottery, cave paintings, ritual urns. Culture also includes the study and practice of highly expressive art forms: painting, sculpture, theater, and literature. Culture understood in its most basic sense, however, is a social group's mental world—the realm of meaning, significance, intention, value—which people produce by their acts, practices, and habits. Most people probably think of culture as what the world around them encourages them to take for granted as true, including what they are to take as true—i.e., as sound or acceptable—about right and wrong.

Those who study cultures try to look at them in what they call a "nonjudgmental" or "value-neutral" way. They strive to bracket questions of truth and genuine moral value. This stance is important in practicing anthropology. Possessing moral convictions about a matter under study— say, ritual human sacrifice—does not disqualify the interpreter. One does not actually have to be a value agnostic to be an anthropologist. But the anthropologist's moral convictions do not really help him to describe a group's practices, and failure to keep his convictions in check might hinder accurate description.

The reader of this book inhabits a culture no less value-laden than that inhabited by those societies described in anthropology class. Readers of this book do not adhere to "cargo cults"; few may be inclined to ghost dancing. (Ghost dancing is not a hip-hop craze; it was a ritual among some Native Americans a long time ago.) But the culture "out there" influences our choosing and acting, often powerfully and sometimes conclusively, just as culture has influenced people across the centuries. We are no more able to choose what can and cannot be brought to our minds as a live option for choice than primitive people could. For example, the vast majority of us cannot believe in magic and astrology because we live in a scientific culture; but for centuries people could hardly avoid believing in magic and astrology, for the world was not explained in any other terms.

Culture can imprison our thoughts, and thus ourselves. In all too many cultures genuine friendship between persons of different races or clans, for example, has been impossible because of false cultural beliefs about the indelible inferiority of some group. Stories as diverse as *Romeo and Juliet* and *Driving Miss Daisy* compellingly explore the difficulties of friendship across ethnic and racial divides. Anthropologists tell us how the British explorer Captain Cook was put to death by Hawaiian natives for acting out of character—not out of character for a famous British explorer, but out of character for the god Lono whose incarnation they took him to be.[38] In many cultures today parents can scarcely regard baby girls as they do baby boys. Their cultures tell them to value their children, not intrinsically, but for what the kids can do—for the nation, for the parents, for the clan. The value imputed to girls is a function of the surrounding culture's prejudices.

What about our main concern, the matter of law and culture? Cultural formations mediate to each one of us the moral realities to which they give expression. (We got a glimpse of this in chapter 1, when we looked at how marriage in law trickles down to the actual marriage of ordinary people.) These patterns of thought and action are crucially affected by the law. For a long time, including the era in which Oliver Wendell Holmes emerged as a great legal figure, American law and culture coexisted peacefully. The "common law" was conceived to be the residue of culture. The law was not any judge's say-so or even the say-so of the judiciary as a body; judicial declarations counted, rather, as evidence of the law. The law itself was the common practice or custom of the people.

Much has changed since Holmes's day. In our day common law has been eclipsed by statutes, executive orders, administrative rules, and judicial activism. The harmonious integration of law, culture, and convention characteristic of the common-law era is over. Law on the one hand and culture and convention on the other have split. The split has engendered what one astute commentator has termed the "chicken-egg" problem.[39] Some people see law as the solution to many cultural ills. These people see law as the driver of culture, as if law could by itself overcome cultural restraints and disorder. They often do not recognize that law depends greatly upon a hospitable cultural environment for its effective reception. When their legal reforms overshoot cultural conditions, the result is disrespect for the law more than anything else. Call these people "reformers from the top down."

Others are "reformers from the bottom up." They would put all their energy into changing culture (including conventional morality) before turning to legal change. They argue that America's permissive abortion laws should not be changed until America's women (and men) have been educated to see that abortion is a choice unworthy of them. "You cannot legislate morality," they say.[40] Abortion should be "safe, legal, and rare." These "reformers from the bottom up" put their faith in education and cultural change. The idea is to shape people so that they neither need nor desire abortions; then they will be ready to accept the legal prohibition of abortion. In this view, law is the trailer, the superstructure, while culture is the cab, the leader.

The idea that education, not law, is the best instrument for social change and reform is one to which most people seem to have surrendered today. But it nonetheless subsists on a mistaken view of how culture relates to law. As Francis Cardinal George recently wrote:

> Law has peculiar and unique cultural functions in American society. . . . The many components of our culture are largely united by law, not by blood, not by race, not by religion, not even by language, but by law. It's the one principal cultural component we all have in common. . . . [L]aw is more important in teaching or instructing us than it is in directing us. . . . [O]ne must therefore ask how it is that law functions as a cultural carrier in [this country], and what does that mean for cultural institutions that are universal [i.e., objective, natural] but that are qualified by law: marriage, family [and others].[41]

The United States Supreme Court has testified to law's profound capacity to shape culture. Affirming the central holding of *Roe v. Wade*,[42] the court wrote in *Planned Parenthood v. Casey* that "[a]n entire generation has come of age free to assume *Roe's* concept of liberty in defining the capacity of women to act in society, and to make reproductive decisions."[43] With what effect? "[F]or two decades . . . people have organized intimate relationships and made choices that define their views of themselves and their places in society, in reliance on the availability of abortion in the event that contraception should fail. The ability of women to participate equally in the economic and social life of the Nation has been facilitated by their ability to control their reproductive lives."[44]

The court in *Casey* was not talking just about the millions of women who had abortions since the procedure was legalized in 1973. The court was talking about how *Roe* altered the psychology and self-understanding, the dreams and achievements, of every woman. All women (according to the court) enjoy the benefits of ultimate "control [over] their reproductive lives." Permissive abortion laws are like unemployment insurance or Medicaid, or any other strand in the social safety net. No matter what chances one takes with one's money or job, no matter how bad one's luck turns, one knows that one is not going to starve or be left to die with no doctor to lend a hand. No matter what choices a woman makes about sexual activity and contraception, she knows that there is always a legally available way to stay competitive on the nation's "economic and social" playing field.

But the *Casey* court was far too passive in the face of a permissive culture (assuming that its understanding of our culture was even accurate). Cultural patterns should count for little when legal security for basic human rights is at issue. The Supreme Court took precisely this view in 1954 when it ruled that racial segregation was unconstitutional. That case—*Brown v. Board of Education*[45]—is widely thought to be the finest moment in the court's history. In deciding that segregation was unconstitutional, the court counted culture for practically nothing. The lawyer defending racial separation—John W. Davis, one of the greatest advocates in the court's history—argued that whether segregation was right or wrong was, by 1954, not the point. Davis said that the moral question about justice was secondary to the fact that a social order was based upon racial separation. Davis referred chiefly but not exclusively to the customs and mores and culture of the South, whose racial caste system had been blessed by the Supreme Court itself in an 1896 case, *Plessy v. Ferguson*.[46] Davis's argument enjoyed the support of the court's precedent. Without denying the cultural fact of the matter, the court unanimously declared that "separate is inherently unequal," that segregation is simply wrong and therefore unconstitutional.

The laws invalidated in *Brown* manifested the racist beliefs of powerful people in those places where segregation was practiced. These laws followed cultural prejudices, to be sure. It might seem, therefore, that reform from the bottom up was the only real chance at effective change. "You can't legislate morality," they say. At the same time laws upholding the South's racial caste system contributed to racist cultural beliefs. "Does anyone doubt for a second," asks one astute writer, "that legally required segregation—with blacks consigned to quarters on the far side of the tracks, drinking from 'colored only' water fountains, and traipsing past whites to the rear of the bus—reinforced, perpetuated, and over time helped to create that culture?"[47] Can anyone reasonably doubt that racist laws structured and sustained a racist culture? And vice versa?

Brown and *Roe* are revealing case studies of the relationship among the objective requirements of justice, positive law, and culture. Neither one, nor both taken together, illustrates all the pertinent considerations and nuances. But they will have to suffice as examples for now. It is time to turn to conventional morality and the challenges it poses to law.

All that we have said about culture and law on matters of basic justice applies to conventional morality. Conventional morality is what people say is the right thing to do. Racial prejudice underlay the conventional morality where segregation was practiced. Racism supported local moral norms, such as "a black man is not permitted to be alone with a white woman, but a white man is permitted to be alone with a black woman." These conventional norms were reflected in positive law. Rape was all but presumed where a white woman complained of a black man's sexual assault, and rarely prosecuted where a black woman complained of a white man's assault. Without legal sanction, it is scarcely imaginable that the South's racial caste system would have survived for as long as it did. We also know from the sad experience with lynching that, in the absence of legal sanctions for "proper" racial etiquette, culture and convention could still have their way. As the example of Atticus Finch in *To Kill A Mockingbird* shows, however, nothing about culture or convention changes the objective requirements of justice: we should treat all others as we would have them treat us.

3. RELIGION, MORALITY, AND THE CONSTITUTION

ESSENTIAL TO ANY ACCOUNT of law's moral foundations—including this one—is a response to a standing constitutional objection. The claim is that our First Amendment separated not only church and state, but also public life from the influence of religious ethics. The claim is one about the meaning of positive law; in this case, it is about interpreting our fundamental law's prohibition on "establishments of religion." This legal claim depends in part, however, on a philosophical contention whose effects are at the heart of this book's concerns. The contention is that "religious ethics" includes any morality that is objective, that is, categorical, universal. This supporting philosophical point is really just an implication of contemporary moral skepticism: since reason cannot supply the grounds for any objective morality, all such moral theories must be products of revelation or religious authority, if they are not just empty or naïve posturing.

There is unfortunately some support in recent decisions of the Supreme Court for this objection and the philosophical assertion upon which it depends. The high court is carrying on a dangerous flirtation with moral subjectivism. The justices can scarcely be counted on to affirm the existence of secure objective moral knowledge when it comes to moral issues such as abortion and marriage. But the court's holdings are erratic and dense and continue to develop in unanticipated ways. The point of this chapter is to show that these holdings—insofar as they do support the objection and its dependents—are wrong. They represent a judicial inversion of our constitutional heritage.

Our constitutional tradition was marked until recently by cooperation between government and religion for the common good of political society, a relationship in which the government favored no religion over others and coerced no one. The tradition affirmed the possibility of an objective moral law, while recognizing that religion supported and sanctioned ethics. Perhaps most important our constitutional tradition regarded the secondary role of religion in sustaining people's belief in objective morality as a welcome, even vital, benefit to the life of political society.

Here is a telling illustration of our constitutional heritage on religion, morality, and law:

At the time our Constitution and Bill of Rights were enacted, much of what is now the upper Midwest was under the direct government of the United States Congress. This area was not composed of states as it now is and as the eastern seaboard was. The whole area, which now includes Ohio, Michigan, Indiana, and Illinois, was then called the Northwest Territory. The Constitution says that Congress shall have power to make "all needful" rules respecting the territories of the United States. Now we have few territories: Puerto Rico, the U.S. Virgin Islands, Guam, American Samoa, and the Federated States of Micronesia. But even as late as 1900 vast stretches of the continental United States were under Congress's control, for example, territory that had been acquired in the 1803 Louisiana Purchase, including a wide area stretching from Montana, Wyoming, Utah, and Arizona in the north and west, to Oklahoma, Arkansas, and Louisiana in the south and Kansas and Missouri in the east.

The basic law that governed the Northwest Territory was called, unsurprisingly, the "Northwest Ordinance." The part of interest to us read like this: "Religion, morality, and knowledge, being necessary to good government and the happiness of mankind, schools and the means of education should forever be encouraged."

That one sentence perfectly expresses our enduring national commitment to cooperation between government and religion for the sake of public morality. It indicates as well how objective morality and positive law were supposed to work together for our good and the good of our country.

This "perfect" sentence was no one-statute wonder. The same formulation was used by the United States Congress many times throughout the nineteenth century; it appeared in other bills called into being to serve as the fundamental law of vast territorial swaths. Generations of congressmen were firmly committed to the propositions expressed in this sentence. Many millions of people lived under the guidance of the Northwest Ordinance and its sentence about religion, morality, and knowledge.

"Religion, morality, and knowledge, being necessary to good government and the happiness of mankind. . . ." Our forefathers firmly believed it was so. And they said let us encourage schools.

In other words, the conclusion of our forefathers was that because religion, morality, and knowledge are essential, it was important to encourage schools. Schools would not only impart knowledge—the three Rs and the like. They would also do something helpful or good concerning religion and morality. The Northwest Ordinance does not literally say that the schools should teach or inculcate religion and morality; that is simply implied in the way it is written. But we can be sure that schools promoted and inculcated knowledge; otherwise, one can scarcely imagine them doing anything. And religion and morality were also included in the schools' mission statement, as we might call it today. No distinction was made; none was evidently intended. Congress expressed a favorable judgment about knowledge and identified the institution tasked with transmitting it to the next generation of citizens. That institution was the school. The Northwest Ordinance implies that Congress made the same judgments about both religion and morality: they are good, and schools should be established to transmit those goods, too, to the next generation. Thus, territorial schools had a tripartite agenda: religion, morality, and knowledge.

We are not talking about parochial schools here, of which there would have been very few—and maybe none—on the frontier. We are talking about publicly supported town schools—public schools.

The Northwest Ordinance was not a wish list of platitudes, or an unfunded mandate concocted for popular consumption. Congress made concrete provisions to bring the benefits of religion, morality, and knowledge to the territories. One lot in each township was reserved for schools, another for religion, usually for the congregation that first offered to actually build a church edifice

"Religion, morality and knowledge." But which morality? It could not be the subjectivist morality of the *Casey* "Mystery Passage," in which what works for you is good for you and your kind, but is not necessarily valid for me. The sentence of the Northwest Ordinance makes no sense whatsoever if morality is subjective. If morality is individualized, what would schools teach to the whole class? If morality is subjective, what possible basis—even what sense—could there be in saying that it is good for people and for government? If morality is subjective then there is no "morality." There are just so many "moralities," and no one could reasonably judge them all good for government. Some surely would not be.

The historical truth is that early American schools taught and inculcated an objective morality—the common morality of Christians and Jews. It was biblical morality, the Ten Commandments, as well as virtuous habits, such as temperance and frugality. The truth is that schools taught these sublime matters well into the twentieth century.

How was this morality related to religion? Some people at the time of the founding thought that one needed religion to know the good, others that one needed to know religion in order to be good. The first group believed that the intellect and character of humans were so corrupted by sin that good and evil appeared to them as gauzy, indistinct alternatives, all the more evanescent because humans were prone to rationalize their sinful ways. What we see in our rearview mirrors we easily convince ourselves is fine, or as good as possible. Religion—more specifically, revelation and its transmission by authoritative teachers (churches)—removed the scales from our eyes.

The second group thought that the human mind, despite the corrupting effects of Adam and Eve's fall from grace, could grasp the truths of morality. Some behavior was known by and through reason to be wrong for everybody, in all places and at all times. Adultery, murder, and bearing false witness were always and everywhere wrong. These things were not wrong because humans had decided to call them wrong, or because some king or legislature said they were wrong. They were and are naturally wrong. These early Americans believed in universal moral norms, knowable—in principle—by unaided human reason. This second group realized, however, that we all needed help to be good. Religion was the greatest of all helps because it promised eternal reward to the righteous, and misery forever to the evil.

The Northwest Ordinance says that three things—religion, morality, and knowledge—are to be taught in schools because they are "necessary" to two other goods: the "happiness of mankind" and "good government." By "happiness" those who enacted the law did not mean gaiety or fun or recreation. They meant integral human flourishing, moral goodness. Our founders are heard to say, flatly and without qualification or embarrassment, that the goodness of people considered by itself is public business. Goodness is not simply private; much less, as we have seen, is it a matter of mere taste or subjective preference. Lawmakers were to have an idea about the constitutive features of human well-being; otherwise, they could not promote "the happiness of mankind." Human well-being comprised, among other things, religion, morality, and knowledge. The founders believed, in other words, that law was *for* persons and the communities in which they could flourish.

"Religion, morality, and knowledge" are also "necessary to good government." The same thought is expressed in the single greatest contribution to political theory ever written by an American—*Federalist* 10. In this essay, James Madison addressed the dependence of what we would call democracy on civil society. Madison said: "Republican government presupposes a virtuous citizenry."[48] Madison knew, as did the other founders, that nondespotic political institutions dedicated to the general welfare were limited in the measures they could adopt to assure that citizens were, in fact, virtuous enough to make the experiment in liberty a success. By encouraging knowledge, morality, and religion through public schools, the founders aimed to preserve and pass on republican virtue.

Here is my restatement of what we have found in the Northwest Ordinance: Religion and morality are part of the good human life. Government should help people to be good. It is essential to the success of good government that people be good. This was, I submit, the view of the overwhelming majority of people in this country—and the guiding public philosophy in this country—until well into the twentieth century. It is still the conviction of many, many Americans.

The Supreme Court rejected this arrangement, root and branch, shortly after World War II, in two cases: *Everson* in 1947 and *McCollum* in 1948. In place of the earlier understanding, the court adopted a new master church-state norm, one that would before long vanquish all traces of religion, and most evidence of objective morality, from public schools. The new rule was binding upon all the nation's governmental bodies, from the United States Congress all the way down to the smallest rural school district in the smallest state. The rule was this: no public authority could aid or promote or encourage religion, even where it would do so without discriminating among religions, and even where no one at all was coerced. The justices said that they were going beyond equality among religions, which, they said was in truth the original meaning of nonestablishment; they would henceforth let no public body prefer religion over "non-religion." No public authority could say or signal in any way that religion is good—for people themselves or for good government or both. To "endorse"—the court's current artful term—religion in this way would violate the Constitution's command of "neutrality."

The new master norm eliminated from public authority's understanding the proposition we found in the Northwest Ordinance, that religion is part of the good human life. This objective moral norm could no longer be a reason for action by public officials, any more than a belief in the inferiority of African Americans could: both were unconstitutional bases for law. With religion already evicted, objective morality was soon in the docks; the acids of secularism soon reduced objective morality to the status of "religious ethics." The new rule also subordinated the free exercise of religion to any appearance or trace of its establishment. Even where, as in the *Everson* case,[49] public assistance to believers—subsidized bus rides for kids to Catholic schools—actually helped them to live out their freely chosen religious commitments, the court struck them down. Maintaining the government's alleged "neutrality" towards religion was more compelling than helping people to be the people they freely chose to be.

Most students of the Constitution agree that it was precisely the other way around all along: nonestablishment was a means or a condition of free exercise. One way that people enjoyed freedom of belief was by being free of compulsory support for and deference to one sect or church. No wonder that John Courtney Murray said of the *Everson* and *McCollum* cases, "The First Amendment [was] stood on its head. And in that position it cannot but gurgle juridical nonsense."[50]

Why did the Supreme Court fifty years ago abandon our constitutional heritage? Why did the justices turn their backs upon the truths found in the Northwest Ordinance? We know that the war against fascism called forth among Americans a profound recommitment to "democracy." During World War II we fought for "the democratic way of life," a political culture with deep roots in character, belief, and psyche. But "democracy" or "democratic theory" was splintered into two camps.

One group held beliefs much like those articulated earlier by Madison: republican government presupposed a virtuous citizenry. The opposing camp after World War II saw moral truth as a phantom, a superstition that, when it possessed citizens' minds, led straight to authoritarianism, if not to outright fascism. This group favored a pragmatic scientific spirit and relativism in morals, and this was the group that won. Thus, we see, right there in the Supreme Court cases during and shortly after the war, an explicit link between our "democratic way of life," even our "democratic faith," and secularism, particularly in public education.

Here is a nice illustration of the point from the oral argument in *McCollum*, which took place on December 8, 1947, just ten months after the shocking *Everson* declaration against any and all government help to religion, even if the help was nondiscriminatory and noncoercive. Justice Frankfurter made this point to John Franklin, lawyer for a school district that permitted, at parents' request, religious instruction of children in the schools:

> I put my question again: we have a school system of the United States on the one hand, and the relation it has to the democratic way of life. On the other hand we have the religious beliefs of our people. The question is whether any kind of scheme which introduced religious teaching into the public school system is the kind of thing we should have in our democratic institutions.

Frankfurter answered his own question: because a few religious groups opposed the school's shared-time program, it was "offensive" and caused "controversy."[51] Its incompatibility with our democracy needed no further proof—at least not for Frankfurter.

Most worthy of notice in Frankfurter's question is the elevation of a political process—democracy—into a cultural system. This new "democratic faith" achieved paramount normative status via the court's authoritative reception of it into the Constitution. The effects have been no less than revolutionary.

4. CRIME AND PUNISHMENT
∂ৎ

THERE ARE SEVERAL USEFUL WAYS in which we can map and visualize the law's domain. In the United States we have demarcated political and thus legal authority along two axes. *Federalism* refers to vertical separation into national, state, local, or municipal authorities, with the law of nations (international law) making its way slowly and sometimes controversially into the picture. *Separation of powers* refers to horizontal distribution of public authority to the legislative, executive, and judicial branches of government.

Another legal map can be visualized as cut into quadrants. The occupants of the quadrant's four corners are constitutions (fundamental law); statutes (what legislatures produce); common law (basically, the law made by courts); and the ever more important realm of administrative agency rules (Internal Revenue Service regulations or environmental rules, for example). Off to the side of this grid again stands international law, occupying a special place of its own.

Law schools present another kind of legal map. The usual course of study looks like a pyramid, with students ascending from a broad base of required survey courses up to ever more concentrated, focused studies—seminars and the like. The first year of study includes the most generally studied subjects: contracts, property law, torts (wrongs), constitutional law, and procedure. The third year is typically composed of "boutique" courses—specialized seminars, internships, and some practical courses, such as trial advocacy.

On any map of the legal world criminal justice occupies a prominent place. It is not quite as prominent as the drawing of Manhattan in the cartoon map of the famous Saul Steinberg poster in the *New Yorker*, the one depicting the West Side in great detail, right down to curbs and fire hydrants on Ninth Avenue, with the world across the Hudson shown as small, blank areas, labeled "Jersey" and "Japan." But it is close.

What is "criminal justice"? It is, first, the law of crimes. In criminal law class students learn how murder is distinguished from the lesser offense of manslaughter. They learn how the various kinds of theft—larceny, robbery, and embezzlement—differ. And they are taught which aggravating factors ratchet up a robbery or burglary or assault from third (the least serious) to first degree.

The study of criminal law is almost universally called mastering the *elements of the offense,* which combination of "act" (plunging the knife into victim's chest), "state of mind" (intentionally), "result" (the victim died), and "surrounding circumstances" (the victim was a police officer) makes a course of action into a specific crime (here, first degree murder of a peace officer).

Interwoven with the various crimes is the distinction between "felony" and "misdemeanor." Felonies are those crimes punishable by more than a year's imprisonment. The universe of felonies is divided further into classes, perhaps "A" through "E," each with a corresponding specified range of punishment. "B" felonies might be punishable by a prison term of up to twenty-five years. Punishment for an "E" felony might be capped at four years.

This part of the law is wholly positive. There is no common law of crimes in the United States; if it is not written down in the statute books and denominated a "crime," then it simply is not a prosecutable offense in this country. Again, if you want to know what is a punishable crime, look it up in the books. Even universal moral condemnation does not make an act into a crime. However, many crimes are among the most morally heinous acts imaginable.

Huge segments of any criminal law class have nothing to do with studying the elements of the offense or sentencing classifications but are rather entirely concerned with morality. These segments include unvarnished, clear statements of what counts as a human act, free choice, moral responsibility, and just desserts. I say that these are "unvarnished" because we are not talking about truncated, refracted legal versions of basically moral ideas. We are talking about the real moral deal. Another important part of criminal law is the question, more philosophical than legal, about criminalizing what are called "victimless immoralities"—recreational drug use, gambling, prostitution, and other sexual improprieties.[52]

A perennial feature of first-year "crime" class is the case of *Regina v. Dudley and Stephens*.[53] Two shipwrecked sailors—the defendants—killed and consumed a sickly cabin boy who was adrift with them in a lifeboat. They reasoned that the boy would likely die before any possible rescue and that, unless they consumed him, they would die too. Dudley and Stephens were indeed rescued. Then they were indicted and subsequently tried for murder. The court convicted them and they were sentenced to hang. The queen later commuted—i.e., reduced, in an act of clemency— their sentences to six months' imprisonment.

Dudley and Stephens is full to the brim with moral lessons. The first has to do with the moral equality of everyone's life before the law. The sickly cabin boy was *in extremis*. He really would have perished soon. No matter. Even if the defendants' dire predictions were true—at least we might be saved but only if we consume the kid—that boy enjoyed the same right to not be killed as did the defendants. The survivors were convicted of murder just as if they had burst into a nursery and gunned down a healthy child.

The second moral lesson reinforces the first. The sailors mounted an unsuccessful "justification" defense. *Justification* refers to a situation in which some act that would be criminal under ordinary circumstances is judged to be good or desirable ("justified") in the particular instance. Standard examples include tearing down a house during a conflagration to halt the spread of a fire, flooding a farmer's land to stall an advancing enemy army, and using deadly force to fend off a rapist. In saying that these acts are *justified* the law is saying that anyone under these circumstances does the right thing by pulling down the house, flooding the farmer's field, or striking the rapist in self-defense.

The third moral lesson has to do with the sailors' failed "excuse" defense. *Excuse* refers to a criminal act that is bad or undesirable. Society does not benefit from the act, and persons in the same circumstances should avoid performing it. But sometimes it is too much to ask people to observe the law. An *excused* person is not held criminally liable. Insanity is one kind of excuse; persons who operate under threats of force or harm are typically excused, too. The court held the two shipwrecked sailors to a high standard of moral responsibility that, even if a bit severe, shows how stern is the stuff of which the criminal law is made.

It is easy to see already how criminal law depends for its justice and its intelligibility upon a solid grasp of basic moral principles and concepts. But what about the central phenomenon, the state's infliction of punishments ranging from fines to imprisonment to death. How is state conduct of that sort morally justified?

Punishment always involves the deliberate imposition by the political community's administrative arm—the state—of some privation or harm upon an unwilling member of the society. Whether punishment takes the form of the rack, or restitution, or time in jail, the question arises,

How is such a grave imposition morally justified? This is the question usually treated in law school as the "point" or "purpose" or "rationale" of punishment. It is typically the first topic in criminal law class.

The laundry list of punishment's purposes in a criminal law casebook includes "deterrence," "rehabilitation," and "incapacitation." These refer to sanctioning a convicted criminal with a view to (respectively) providing a disincentive to others to commit similar crimes; making the criminal well; and isolating the prisoner from law-abiding people. The problem is that, while these purposes may be legitimate secondary aims of punishment, none provides a moral justification for punishing anyone. Only "retribution" does that. But retribution is largely neglected in the law schools. Where it is mentioned, retribution is almost always misunderstood.

Here is a leading example of the neglect and misunderstanding of the concept of retribution. Supreme Court Justice Anthony Kennedy caused a stir at the 2003 meeting of the American Bar Association with pointed comments about punishment that elicited a major response by the ABA, the "Report of the Kennedy Commission." Kennedy's speech was widely hailed as insightful, a clarion call to collective action. To put it mildly, he struck a responsive chord.

Justice Kennedy was nonetheless way off the mark. He said, at one point, that punishment was needed to "vindicate the law, to acknowledge the suffering of the victim, and to deter future crimes. Still, the prisoner is a person; still he or she is part of the family of humankind." A little later in his talk Justice Kennedy acknowledged that the "debate over the goals of sentencing is a difficult one." Then he added,

> Prevention and incapacitation are often legitimate goals. Some classes of criminals commit scores of offenses before they are caught, so one conviction may reflect years of criminal activity. There are realistic limits to efforts at rehabilitation. We must try, however, to bridge the gap between proper skepticism about rehabilitation on the one hand and improper refusal to acknowledge that the more than two million inmates in the United States are human beings . . . .[54]

In these few sentences Kennedy propounded a host of confusions about punishment. He silently bypassed, for example, the fundamental question: what morally justifies drastic impositions upon the two million incarcerated Americans? He used the term "goal," not the concept of moral justification. He thereby suggested that the question had to do with a nonevaluative means/end test of efficiency, or something technical such as we saw in chapter 1 with "good" and "bad" baseball players. Kennedy then placed in opposition two kinds of "goals": "prevention" and "incapacitation" on the one hand, and "rehabilitation" on the other. Next he implicitly asserted that rehabilitation "acknowledge[s]" the prisoner's humanity, and that "prevention" and "incapacitation" do not. Kennedy surely seemed to be saying that "prevention" and "incapacitation" sacrifice the prisoner's human dignity. He nonetheless added that "prevention" and "incapacitation" are "often" "legitimate goals." Kennedy said nothing about retribution.

The problem is that none of Kennedy's goals, even broadly construed, is the central moral justification for punishing criminals. Deterrence, rehabilitation, incapacitation, "redemption," and reconciliation (of victim and offender) are, at most, secondary aims of punishment. Without retribution at the center, these ends simply do not justify punishing anyone.

Let's talk about retribution, first by clarifying some misconceptions about it. Retribution is not *lex talionis*, the law of retaliation, "an eye for an eye."[55] To apply the "eye for an eye" norm literally, organized communities would have to be prepared, logistically as well as morally, to do anything that their most depraved individual members had done. I doubt that any society has lowered its moral standards to that of its most depraved criminals. It is true that "eye for an eye" is found in the Bible. But we are given reason by scripture scholars to believe that "eye for an eye" was meant to limit retaliatory acts to no more than the loss incurred, which logically does not imply or entail a command to exact at least that.

Retribution is not about domesticating popular hatred for a known criminal. It is not about channeling repugnance towards a particularly heinous crime. It is not revenge. Retribution is not driven by anger, hatred, or any other emotion; as such, it is completely distinct from community outrage.

Retribution has little (if anything) to do with the "intrinsic value" of inflicting suffering on wrongdoers, as the legal philosopher H. L. A. Hart suggested it does.[56] That Hart considered suffering to have "intrinsic value" is troubling. Suffering is necessarily a privation, a loss, a difficulty, a subtraction from the way things ought to be. Suffering so described is bad, and by definition, something bad does not have "intrinsic value." If it did, it would be good. It seems likely that what Hart actually had in mind was the fact that we feel relieved to see the unjust "pay" for their crimes. Yet that view refers to suffering's instrumental value, not its intrinsic significance.

Retribution tells us little about what a particular defendant's sentence ought to be. Legislative and judicial authorities necessarily (and rightly) make important choices in sentencing criminals about fairness and proportionality, governed by a sense of the sentence's aptness to the crime and its coherent position within the global pattern of possible sentences. In other words, while moral reflection can tell us that assault and theft should be treated as crimes, it cannot tell us which privations should be imposed for those crimes. The sentence for a specific offender is not directly deducible from any single factor; it necessarily involves a decision guided but not dictated by reason.

So what is retribution? Retribution is about equality and fairness among people living under law, properly understood, in political society. In the absence of any established political order, people would do whatever they pleased. Their choices would not necessarily result in a society dominated by uncontrollable selfishness, as Hobbes anticipated.[57] Absent political order, some people would act reasonably, maybe even altruistically, and seek cooperation to achieve common benefit. But there would be no means by which that cooperation could be structured; each person would have to exercise personal judgment about the appropriate way to cooperate with others. Political society, by contrast, provides an authoritative scheme for structuring cooperation, a scheme that thereby excludes all reasonable alternatives. Under such a system, individuals naturally accept restrictions on the freedom to rely on their own personal judgments about successful cooperation.

We have already talked about this distinctive contribution of law to social order in the context of highway speed limits. Consider one more simple illustration. Neither driving on the left side of the road nor on the right is immoral. Either could easily be chosen as the rule of the road. Both cannot be chosen without disastrous consequences, however. Refraining from all authoritative choice would be just as catastrophic. After determining that drivers should stay to the right, political authority may then appropriately penalize those who continue to drive on the left. Legal norms such as this one guide people by specifying the exact form that fair cooperation with others should take; they make general moral obligations concrete and explicit. "Drive in an orderly fashion" includes an obligation to yield to cars and pedestrians in the right of way. The law tells people how to determine who has the right of way under certain conditions. In short, specific legal norms tell people how to effectively treat others fairly.

The important thing is that, once positive law is up and running, justice requires individuals to accept the pattern of liberty and restraint specified by political authorities. Everyone is under a duty of justice to everyone else to put aside the liberty they would have in a "state of nature," even the liberty they would enjoy in a different legal order. By accepting the established apparatus of political society and by observing its requirements, liberty for all is equalized.

Criminal acts often involve injustice to one or a few individuals: the defrauded old lady, the black-and-blue battered spouse, the hapless pedestrian whose car was hijacked. But not always: many crimes are "victimless," where no one in particular is singled out for special harm. Sometimes the harm is specific but diffuse: treason, lying under oath before Congress, and tax evasion. Sometimes the harm is to a collective good such as public morality or public peace: brawling in the streets, public lewdness, gambling, or raucous parties. But what always occurs in crime is this: the criminal usurps the liberty to pursue his own plans and projects in his own way, notwithstanding the law's pattern of restraint. On consideration, what we see in the case of crime is that the entire community remains within the law, each member denying to himself the liberty to do as he pleases, except for the criminal. The criminal acts out. The central wrong in crime, therefore, is not that a criminal causes harm to a specific individual. It is that the criminal unfairly claims the right to pursue his own interests and plans in a manner contrary to the common boundaries delineated by the law. From this perspective, the entire community—save the criminal—is victimized by crime. The criminal's act of usurpation is unfair to everyone else; he has gained an undue advantage over those who remain inside the legally required pattern of restraint.[58]

The goal of punishment is to undo the criminal's bold and unjust assertion of his will. The essence of punishment is to impose upon the prisoner's will, making him suffer some deprivation of the liberty to do as he pleases. The essence of punishment is the restriction of a criminal's will by depriving him of the right to be the sole author of his own actions. Punishment restores the fundamental fairness and equality of mutual restraint that have been disturbed by the criminal's act. Viewed over the course of a criminal's punishment—say, the duration of his imprisonment—his usurpation is effaced, undone by being imposed upon. Society is eventually restored to the status quo ante: the equality of mutual restraint within law is finally—again, morally speaking—made whole. The criminal's debt to society is paid.

It is worth remembering that there is a great common benefit—a common good, really—in maintaining within society respect for law, and in fostering the attitude of restraint and self-subordination that law-abidingness entails. Lawbreaking undermines these great common goods. Lawbreaking disadvantages every member of society by devaluing a habit or attitude that is essential to fairness, equality, and social order.

We can now see why prosecutions in our country always list the whole community as the complaining or aggrieved party. In the United States the complaining party is always the political community, styled as "State" or "People" or "Commonwealth," as in *The People of the State of New York v. John Jones*. British criminal prosecutions, by contrast, begin with *Regina* or *Rex*—"Queen or King"—and reflect the traditional British view that criminal offenses are first and foremost offenses against the monarch's peace.

Another indication of how retribution explains and justifies punishment has to do with a perennial chestnut of "crime" classes. The question of punishing the innocent to save others is one of the great challenges of punishment theory. What if a public authority could stave off riots and mayhem only by hanging an innocent person popularly believed to be guilty? Where retribution forms the moral justification for punishment, the problem of punishing the innocent is resolved simply and satisfactorily.

Aside from retribution, all the goals of punishment could be accomplished regardless of specific antisocial acts by the condemned; their goals could in fact be served by punishing the innocent. Under a theory of deterrence, for example, it is impossible to argue that one who is innocent must not be sacrificed to demonstrate the law's fury, if general peace could thereby be secured. The administration of punishment, whether upon the guilty or innocent, necessarily achieves the desired end of deterrence. If we consider rehabilitation in either its therapeutic or moral sense, one can scarcely argue that the law's ministrations must be limited only to those justly convicted of a crime. Some people need moral or psychological help, quite apart from any criminal misbehavior. If we aim to simply isolate or incapacitate dangerous persons, we could wait until they actually hurt someone before we lock them up and throw away the key. But why should we wait? At least in some cases we can see ahead of time that an individual is a walking time bomb before any danger actually arises. And as our psychological diagnostic abilities improve, we may soon be confident that violent acts are better prevented by anticipating them, and therefore we may move to quarantine those who pose a threat to the law-abiding. From all of these perspectives, the line between guilt and innocence could be traversed in pursuit of the state's objectives. That line will therefore sometimes seem an arbitrary barrier, which only the scrupulous or feckless dare not cross.

The aim of retribution, however, is always frustrated— and never served—by punishing the innocent. Punishing someone who has committed no offense is, within a retributive framework, counterproductive. If a person has not distorted society's equilibrium by committing a criminal act, harming him cannot restore that equilibrium. Making an innocent disgorge his bold act of will is simply impossible, for there is nothing to be disgorged. Punishing the innocent is not punishment, but oppression, a new disturbance of equality within society. Punishing the innocent further allows the real criminal, where some crime has been committed, to run free, while also allowing his usurpation of liberty to remain unredressed.

CONCLUSION

No single book, and certainly not this slender volume, could unfailingly guide the student to and through all the pathways where law and morality intersect. But those crossroads are unquestionably the most important junctions in *any* contemporary effort to study law.

Today's law schools supply all the information one could desire about laws. Today's law classroom is full of talk about this or that people's moral convictions. And any law library is full of books about "law and morality." But on the centrally important matter of how to integrate a critically justified morality with a healthy recognition of human law's positivity, there is very little of genuine value indeed. This guide has been intended to fill that gap.

But where this guide is silent, where is the student to turn? One place is the past. In *very* general terms, the bottom fell out of our understanding of law and morality some time shortly after 1960. Note well: "very general terms" means that, while significant strands of misguided thought flourished then (that of Holmes, for example), mainstream reflection and practice fruitfully integrated religion, morality, and laws and this orientation can be discovered in the old books and judicial opinions. Read them and—in very general terms—*ignore* your professors' revisionist interpretations of them.

Read also the increasing number of authors who have stepped into the void to revive and refurbish the tradition: Robert George, Hadley Arkes, Mary Ann Glendon, Russell Hittinger, and John Finnis to name just a few. Where else can the law student turn? To his or her colleagues in the study of law, for our law schools are increasingly populated by students unimpressed by Holmes's skepticism, uninterested in their aging professors' recycled radicalism, and unwavering in their own belief in an objective morality (in some cases they are even sustained by traditional religious doctrines). To these law students, the message is this: find each other, confide in each other, learn from each other, and grow in wisdom together.

APPENDICES
❦

Appendix A: Moral Neutrality

The whole point of chapter 1 is to illustrate the deep inward—that is, self-referential, consensus-driven—turn at the "bottom" or foundation of our legal order: when it comes to what law is *for*, our lawmakers have made consensus the polity's summum bonum. The problem is that, on the debit side of the political ledger, we find gross injustices such as abortion and the contemporary assault upon marriage. The inward turn is meant to reduce potential social divisions over important moral questions. It is rather more likely, however, that the turn has increased division, as the festering discord over *Roe v. Wade* suggests. In any event, the leading edge of the inward turn is the signature doctrine of modern liberalism: "neutrality" about what constitutes a flourishing human life. What is truly good for people is, under the influence of this aspect of liberalism, considered an illegitimate basis for law.

Let us take the matter of marriage to show how liberal "neutrality" works, and at the same time to demonstrate its limits. Many people say that they personally believe marriage is a union of one man and one woman. Many such people are married to persons of the opposite sex, and cannot really imagine the attraction some persons have for others of the same sex. They would be vastly disappointed if one of their children decided that he or she wanted to marry someone of the same sex. They often also say, however, that it would be wrong, perhaps even a grave injustice, for the state to base its law of marriage on a controversial moral judgment, including the judgment—in fact, theirs and that of most people—that marriage is the union of one man and one woman. The thought is that the state ought to be neutral between competing understandings of what marriage is. It would be wrong, these persons say, for the state to impose anyone's moral code for marriage by making it the template all must follow.

This way of looking at marriage, and the public debate surrounding it, suffers from a fatal case of "transparency." As we discussed in the text, people do not really mean that the warrant for their view about marriage (or almost any other moral question) is the fact that the view is theirs. They mean that they hold a certain view on the basis of reasons that they credit and affirm. So far considered, then, the neutrality doctrine acquires whatever validity it has by piggybacking on the transparency problem. Once one sees through "transparency," though, there is no reason to adopt the neutrality doctrine.

Sometimes the classic liberal viewpoint is elaborated along the following lines: Marriage is in truth the union of a man and a woman. Marriage is a sacrament (or an analogous sacred relationship) in many religions. But, though it is the truth about marriage, the religious provenance of this definition makes it an inappropriate basis for civil law. Along these lines, one could say that marriage really is permanent; divorce is impermissible or even, strictly speaking, impossible. But one could coherently say as well that civil law ought not to track this view by making no provision for divorce.

This is wrong, too. To the extent that the classic statement of liberal neutrality about marriage implies that monogamy or gender complementarity, for example, can be shown to be essential to marriage only by revelation or reliance upon religious authorities, the classic statement is simply wrong. Almost all human societies have come to understand marriage as the procreative union of man and woman, regardless of the religious beliefs circulating in those societies.

How about the proposition that marriage ought to be defined in a "neutral" way? Well, "neutrality" between the view that the law ought to prescind from the truth of the matter about marriage, and the view that the law should not prescind from the truth about marriage, is logically impossible. In other words, one cannot rely upon any "neutrality" principle to decide the question, should the law of marriage be neutral? This does not by itself mean that state neutrality when it comes to marriage must be rejected. It simply means that the correctness of the view in favor of practical neutrality must be argued for; simply saying "neutrality" won't do the job.

Sophisticated proponents of moral neutrality argue that the best understanding of political morality for our society requires that the law be morally neutral with respect to marriage. They argue that "alternative understandings of political morality, insofar as they fail to recognize the principle of moral neutrality, are . . . mistaken and ought, as such, to be rejected."[59]

But note well: the claim that the law ought to be morally neutral about marriage, or anything else for that matter, is itself a moral claim. It—the claim that the law ought to be neutral—is not morally neutral. As Professor Robert George points out, anyone who holds that the civil provisions governing marriage, or any other institution or practice, ought to be morally neutral does not assert, nor does the position presuppose, that the law ought to be neutral in determining whether law should be neutral when deciding between competing moral views.[60] It is "obvious," he says, "that neutrality between neutrality and non-neutrality is logically impossible."[61]

APPENDIX B: PRIVACY, ETC.

There are several ways in which moral disagreement as a fact about society can and should—even must—be taken into account by prudent lawmakers. But prudent lawmakers will take account of moral disagreement without succumbing to moral subjectivism. Unlike the Supreme Court in the *Casey* case, prudent lawmakers will explore the ways in which liberty can and must be founded upon objective moral norms.

Sometimes the law navigates around moral disagreement by declaring a matter to be *private*. *Privacy* means that a decision or activity is simply none of the law's business. Saying that a decision—say, whom one should marry—is none of the law's business steers clear of both endorsement and condemnation. Your choice of spouse is simply your business.

Our society's talk about privacy over the last generation or so has often centered upon keeping the police out of one's bedroom. More broadly it has had to do with leaving people alone. Again, leaving everyone alone no more implies a uniform positive or negative moral evaluation of what different persons are doing than leaving everyone alone on a subway car implies a uniform approval of their reading material—which could include *War and Peace*, *MAD* magazine, *Playboy*, or anything else.

Griswold v. Connecticut is the 1965 Supreme Court decision that launched our contemporary doctrine of "privacy."[62] It is a case ostensibly about contraception, specifically, a challenge to a state law—the last of a once common type—that made the distribution of contraceptives illegal. The court's members produced a set of chaotic opinions, but the result was clear enough: the law was unconstitutional. *Griswold* is nevertheless a good illustration of how privacy—properly understood—can help us transcend moral disagreement.

The justices steered clear in *Griswold* of saying that there was a constitutional right to use contraceptives, including within marriage. The center of gravity of the case was marital privacy. It comprises, the justices said, the confidentiality which marital friendship requires for its enjoyment and the spatial privacy in one's home that such friendship requires. The court's opinions refer to the "intimate relation of husband and wife"; "privacy surrounding the marriage relationship"; and, finally, this understanding of marriage: "a coming together for better or worse, hopefully enduring, and intimate to the degree of being sacred."[63] The court's stated focus was not a particular sex act or contraceptives as such. The opinions in the case refrained from expressing judgments—favorable or unfavorable—about the morality of contraception.

People with different moral views on nonmarital sex or other moral matters can live together in political society. We do in America. But our success at living together requires that the state not morally endorse immoral acts or relationships. Two people who cannot agree on the morality of, say, some racy magazines can readily agree that an adult reading them is none of the state's business. Two people who contend over the truth about religion can also agree that the state is not the rightful arbiter of their dispute. And so people can live together in disagreement if the law steers clear of endorsing or otherwise implicitly attributing positive moral value to acts that, in truth, are morally worthless.

Courts and other lawmakers sometimes try to avoid controversial moral judgments by declaring a certain encompassing area (the bedroom) or uncontroversial class of acts (what two consenting adults do privately) to be none of the state's business. One could disagree about that judgment, and about the scope of privacy generally. But those disagreements, however spirited, are not (perhaps unsolvable) first-order disputes about sexual morality. They are disputes about the scope of the political common good, the limits of effective state action, and about the meaning of particular constitutional provisions. And it is precisely by shifting a debate over to less controversial—at least, not morally supercharged—matters of political prudence that we navigate around moral shoals.

It is absolutely essential, however, that lawmakers recognize the limits of this technique for avoiding controversy. As we have seen throughout this book, up to and including appendix A, law is *for* justice, which means that the law must correctly identify subjects of justice—persons—and do justice to their most important communities—the family rooted in marriage and religious societies. On these foundational matters, the pursuit of consensus leads straight to fundamental injustice.

Another means of navigating moral disagreement without collapsing into subjectivism is captured by what we call "tolerance." "Tolerance" is a close relative of privacy. When public authority "tolerates" a certain behavior, it means that, though the tolerated act could be prohibited without injustice, people are at liberty to do as they please. "Tolerance" signals that the act is undesirable and perhaps immoral, and that at some level of principle it would not be wrong for the state to try to discourage the act.

In the history of Western political thought, church-state relations have been the theater upon which "toleration" has played out in tension with the concept of "rights." For centuries political rulers were said to "tolerate" certain religious groups, implying that suppressing or at least discriminating against those religions would be right—that is, just. By the time of our founding and thereafter in other countries, religious liberty was said to be a "right": it would be wrong for the state to suppress any religion, save where putatively religious acts broke out into civil disorder.

"Toleration" reflects the judgment that attempting to discourage the act would, all things considered, probably do more harm than good. Various immoralities presenting little or no harm to nonconsenting people—recreational use of marijuana, some sexual misbehavior, gambling, in some places prostitution—have gradually been decriminalized for this reason: authorities judge that enforcing prohibitions would do more harm than good. This is probably the thinking behind the constitutional repeal of Prohibition in 1933.

A third prudent lawmaking technique promotes a measure of individual autonomy, but again does so without corrupting the state's understanding of what truly is morally valuable. Pornography is an example. Many people today defend pornography as harmless or even helpful to some people. These judgments are of recent vintage; even where pornography had previously been tolerated, it was condemned as morally vicious.

Today pornography is legally available for reasons that go beyond the "tolerance" we just described, and beyond concerns about the limits of law enforcement. This reason has to do with prudential calculations about who would make the judgment call. One who judges that certain magazines and videos are salacious could still judge that the law ought not to interfere with the market for them among consenting adults. Without in any way retreating from an objective moral condemnation of pornographic materials, one could judge that authorizing the state to make the judgment about which books to ban presents a greater risk of harm to the community than the books themselves.

This judgment of lesser and greater evils is not dictated by logic but by experience. It depends upon local circumstances and prudential judgments about, among other matters, how widespread the demand for such worthless materials is; what the supply would be in the absence of legal action; the costs of legal regulation and the likelihood of ever obtaining criminal convictions from juries against pornographers; the judgment and character of those public officials who would be charged with judging which materials to ban; and the potential effectiveness of cultural sanctions against pornography in case efforts at legal control are abandoned.

APPENDIX C: *Determinatio*

An apparently paradoxical property of positive law is that it can make morally binding today what was a matter of moral indifference yesterday. One day county residents are free to burn leaves out of doors. The next day they are not. Laws generally operate this way: on the effective date of a new law the legal and therefore moral obligations of those within the jurisdiction change—just because of what someone in charge did or said.

The leaf-burning example suggests that the source of a citizen's obligations is the lawmakers' will, that someone's say-so is what matters. Call this "legal voluntarism." But lawmaking arises, not from legislators' or judges' wills or from their personal identity or attributes, but from their office and the moral requirements of cooperation in political society. There is a strong moral reason for having within the community someone, or some body, with the responsibility and authority to change the pattern of social cooperation for the common good.

The county resident staring at a yard full of leaves experiences the same temptation as did our highway driver, the temptation to break a law that seems to be an arbitrary imposition, an unwelcome constraint unmoored from any real moral necessity. After all, our driver reasoned, it cannot be wrong to drive seventy-five miles per hour; if it were everyone out west and in Germany would be acting immorally. Our county resident similarly reasons: it cannot be wrong to burn leaves out of doors, for if it were we would all have been acting immorally until yesterday.

Breaking the law is alluring not only where it promises convenience to us, or where it allows us to achieve our goals more efficiently. We sometimes want to break the law to achieve lofty aims. Sometimes, although quite rarely, breaking the law is morally if not legally justified. But the looming presence of great moral principles right there, at the edges and behind and beneath the law, is a standing temptation to the well-intentioned to step outside the line, to break the law. Citizens reason this way often enough. The necessary corrective is found in chapters 2 and 4, in which we discovered the point and value of cooperating with others by and through forbearance according to law.

Now it is time to consider how the same temptation affects those who exercise public authority. It is all too common for police officers who honestly wish to do their jobs—to protect citizens from criminal depredations—to "take the law into their own hands" in order to do so. They sometimes ignore or violate legal provisions intended to protect suspects from search or interrogation for the greater moral good of convicting the bad and protecting the good. Perhaps this has happened with some military police and their handling of suspected terrorists. (It goes without saying that police officers are often accused unjustly of lawbreaking by those who perhaps do not fully understand the requirements of the officers' difficult positions.) Judges are sorely tempted by greater moral principles, too, and Supreme Court justices most of all. We saw earlier how the *Roe* court relied upon an assertion of what the pertinent moral good—"privacy," as the justices saw it—should mean for pregnant women. This same judicial creativity has spawned a war in legal scholarship over what it means for a judge to interpret and apply the Constitution. Justice Scalia and other "originalists" charge that harmful "judicial activism" is little more than judicial philosophizing, of judges reaching through the constitutional text and grabbing hold of some ulterior moral principle. The basic concept that needs to be formally introduced in order to clarify these debates is *determinatio*. Here is how it works: The pivotal distinction is that between norms, rules, or standards on the one hand—all of which are specific enough to actually guide decisions in concrete cases—and principles on the other. A norm or rule or standard capable of guiding a decision is annexed to the description of an act: this act—described thus and so—must not (or must be or may be) done (under the following conditions, by these specified persons), all for the sake of some broader and more important principle.

A "principle" is a justification for a norm. So, for example, the Fifth Amendment contains a norm having to do with an act, i.e., compelling one to be a witness against oneself, and a directive: it is not to be done. This norm can be subsumed under one or more principles—that it is unfair to make one the instrument of one's own indictment, or to make one choose from among contempt, perjury, or conviction. The Fourth Amendment says that no warrant may issue, save upon certain conditions. This norm concretizes a broader, justificatory principle we find preceding it in the text: no unreasonable searches or seizures. And perhaps that is a specification of a very broad principle or value—call it privacy. Another example, the rule against hearsay, is a specification of the norm that precludes unreliable testimony, all to ensure that there is, in principle, a fair trial.

The move from principle to norm is not deductive, nor is it a matter of drawing a compelled inference. The move is much freer, more creative, than that. The move from principle to norm is guided by reason, not determined by reason. In reality, a broad range of possible specifications—corresponding to the universe of act descriptions and to the menu of evaluative directives—are all more or less consistent with a given principle or cluster of principles. (Think again of our driver, and of the Eisenhower administration's decision to build the interstate highway system.) A relatively small number of imaginable specifications will be ruled out as entirely unreasonable, as simply incompatible with the governing principle.

But note that one who moves from principle to norm is exercising a legislative-like authority. One who moves back from norm to principle, and stands there with norm production in mind, has (re)claimed a legislative-like prerogative. When the context is constitutional, the stakes are higher. One who goes behind the text to embrace what one asserts to be its animating values or goals, or to deal anew with the evils that called forth the textual response, stands in the framers' shoes. One who does so is set to write the Constitution anew. It is as if the court felt itself bound only by the broad purposes of government—liberty, prosperity, defense—found in the Preamble to our Constitution. It is as if the court believed that the justices were authorized to fashion constitutional law for our times out of the justices' own views of good public policy.

This is the philosophical ground beneath well-founded concerns about "judicial activism." It is not so much about judicial philosophizing as it is about judicial usurpation of legislative authority, and even of the people's authority to author the Constitution under which they will live.

APPENDIX D: CONFLICTS IN CONSCIENCE BETWEEN MORALITY AND LAW

One objection to locating law's foundations in objective morality is that it inevitably shortchanges the positivity of legal norms. The objection is that morality will elbow out positive law in the interest of conscience, and the great benefits of legal order will be lost.

The short answer is that nothing in objective morality requires the analyst, or the person who is deliberating and choosing and acting, to deny the positivity of law. Everyone can and should distinguish the intra-systemically valid laws of a particular community from the requirements of critical morality.

The common objection to locating law's foundations in objective morality deserves a further response, which is included here in answer to the question, Can a judge who believes in an objective moral order render judgment in accord with positive law even when the positive law in question is unjust? The answer is yes. The judge can and should distinguish the law of a particular community from the requirements of justice. This limited positivism is a matter of separating what counts as law here or there from what is simply right, true, just. And such a distinction distinguishes between where the law comes from and what anyone, all things considered, may—or must—do.

Does critical morality say that a judge's duty is to give judgment according to the natural law in cases of conflict between morality and positive law? No, the question of how much legislative authority a judge is given for the purpose of translating the demands of critical morality into positive law, by nullifying positive law that he believes to be unjust, is a question of positive law, not of morality. Different political systems reasonably differ, both in theory and practice, as to how much legislative authority they confer upon judges. If, for example, a particular judge's views about duty make him a "positivist," his positivism does not place him in conflict with the natural law.

Judges are under the same obligation of truth-telling that applies to the rest of us. If positive law is in conflict with morality, the judge may not lie about it. If his duty is to give judgment according to positive law, then he must either (1) do so or (2) recuse himself. If he can give judgment according to immoral positive law without rendering himself formally or unfairly materially complicit in its immorality, and without giving scandal, then he may licitly do so, though he may also licitly recuse himself. If not, then he must recuse himself.

Let us take the case of abortion and the example of Justice Scalia, whom we will suppose believes that abortion is immoral, and that permissive abortion laws are unjust. He holds that the Constitution has nothing to say about abortion. If Indiana restricted or prohibited abortion, it would be free to do so just as California would be free to introduce abortion-on-demand. If Justice Scalia honestly believes that the Constitution fails to protect unborn persons, as he evidently does believe, he is obliged by morality not to lie about it. If lying is permissible for, say, good or proportionate reasons, a judge holding the view that abortion is tantamount to murder could justify, to himself, some false assertion about the meaning of the Constitution in order to avoid the unjust consequences of an honest statement of his views about the positive law. But unjust laws are laws nonetheless, though they do not bind in conscience the way just laws do; and if the judge's honest opinion about the relevant legal materials is that permissive abortion laws are constitutionally permissible, then that is that.

The alternatives to giving judgment, according to positivist law, are to recuse oneself from the case or to resign the office. Either move should be accompanied by a clear public statement of the reasons for doing so: the people who trusted one with judicial responsibility are entitled to be told why this exercise of the judicial office is one that cannot, in good conscience, be performed.

APPENDIX E: "YOU CAN'T LEGISLATE MORALITY"

Law cannot make people good. Law is concerned mainly with external behavior, and not with those matters of the heart (and will and intention) which distinguish persons who are truly good from conformists and timeservers. The law says that one must give testimony when subpoenaed to trial. The law does not care whether you come and testify only to gain attention, with no desire to make a contribution to society. The law does not care why you keep your hands to yourself. The law cares only that you do so.

On the other hand, nothing can really make a person good. People have to make themselves into good persons. They can do so by doing the right thing for the right reason. No one can do that for another, any more than one person can profess religious faith for another. Law can, on the other hand, help people to make themselves good. As Robert George has written, laws prohibiting certain vices, especially of the sexual kind, can help people establish for themselves a virtuous character by (1) preventing the continued self-degradation that follows habitual immoral activity; (2) forestalling the bad example that performance of immoral acts unmolested by law supplies to others; (3) "helping to preserve the moral ecology in which people make their morally self-constituting choices," which we have mostly called law's support for a morally decent culture; and (4) "educating people about moral right and wrong."[64]

Does Professor George propose to legally enforce moral duties across the board? Certainly not. No one in American politics has thought that law should reproduce morality. One reason for this is the Christian faith that has shaped our culture and its laws from the time of the very first Puritan settlement in Massachusetts. Christianity involves moral duties on the part of believers, to God, to one another, and to the community of believers, which have never been, essentially, the state's business. In other words, Christians have always insisted that the church and not the state directs people towards the good life.

There is nonetheless a lively debate today about what is usually called "legal moralism." We have seen glimpses of it in our discussion of the "transparency" problem and the *Lawrence* case, to cite just two examples. This debate grows ever more heated as the moral consensus about the wrongness of certain "victimless immoralities" wanes, and as, under the influence of the *Casey* "Mystery Passage," morality is increasingly viewed as subjective.

The "victimless immoralities" debate started in its current form in 1957, when a blue-ribbon commission headed by Sir John Wolfenden recommended to the British Parliament that it decriminalize private homosexual behavior between consenting adults. Much the same argument has since taken place—and continues to occur—over other consensual sexual immoralities, recreational drug use, prostitution, and some forms of gambling.

The "Wolfenden Report" ignited the most celebrated

jurisprudential debate of the twentieth century, which involved a series of scholarly exchanges between Oxford legal philosopher H. L. A. Hart and High Court Judge Patrick Devlin.[65] The report's specific proposal about sodomy rested upon a controversial and sweeping claim: "It is not the duty of the law to concern itself with immorality as such."[66]

Devlin's basic criticism was that there could be no "theoretical" limit to the reach of the law; no act could be said to be, a priori and as a matter of principle, none of the law's business.[67] H. L. A. Hart, while saying little directly in favor of the "Wolfenden Report's" reasoning, attacked Devlin's position. Hart said that if the "no-theoretical limit" claim is taken as either an empirical assertion or as a necessary truth, it is false. Societies routinely survive changes in the basic moral views of their members. It is absurd to suppose, Hart concluded, that when such a change occurs, we must say one society has disintegrated, and another has succeeded it.[68]

It is important to stress that while Devlin is routinely seen as the "conservative" and "traditionalist" in the exchange, he is so only in a restricted sense. For Devlin rejected the possibility of an objective morality; he was conservative in his social theory, but not in morals. Devlin criticized the traditional claim that law ought to inculcate virtue as "not acceptable to Anglo-American thought. It . . . destroys freedom of conscience and is the paved road to tyranny."[69] In fact, Devlin embraced a (limited) noncognitivism about ethics: basic moral truths are inaccessible to reason. In this he was very much in line with the philosopher David Hume.

We can now appreciate that Devlin meant to say that no particular type or category of act could ever be said to be "in principle" (a priori, or categorically) incapable of posing a threat to social cohesion. Any action—eating meat, eating fish, polygamy, and monogamy—might subvert a moral commitment around which people have integrated themselves, thus constituting a society. Morals laws are justified, Devlin argued, to protect society against the disintegrating effects of actions that undermine a society's constitutive morality—whatever it might be. Whether it is helpful to think of this position as "conservative" is doubtful.

I do not think that this dispute—the dispute about non-interference with immoralities—is entirely settled. There are, however, several points of broad agreement. Very few people hold that there are no limits to the political community's role in enforcing morality. There is, in other words, broad agreement that the political common good does not embrace all the good that can be pursued by people working in concert. The division of opinion in this area is principally whether law should limit itself to a concern with preventing tangible harms to nonconsenting third parties, or whether there is a public morality—a moral ecology—which public authority may rightly promote. There is also broad practical agreement that putatively "victimless" immoralities, like prostitution and drug abuse, have such significant negative effects upon society as a whole that legal regulation of these activities, while not altogether uncontroversial, is not going to end anytime soon. That is, while the arguments in support of these regulations may differ significantly—and they do, as we shall see—that these activities call for legal regulation is a widely shared conclusion.

Appendix F: Positivism and Natural Law

Discussion of law's moral foundations has often been cast as a debate between "natural lawyers" and "positivists." The question was classically put this way: "Is there a necessary connection between law and morality?" Natural lawyers were supposed to answer yes; positivists, no.

The battle has largely been the product of misunderstanding. The parties to the two opposing sides could have agreed for the most part on an answer, and that largely because the focal points of the theories—natural law and positivism—are different. Natural law theory does not purport to be about the law of a particular community. Natural law theory purports to provide the resources necessary to morally evaluate the laws of all communities. Natural law theorists have never claimed that law should reproduce morality. Thomas Aquinas, for example, held for good reasons that only the more grievous immoralities, chiefly those harmful to others, should be legally interdicted. No natural lawyer has ever opined that all laws promulgated by public authorities actually were just.

Positivism originated in the work of John Austin. Austin aimed to develop an understanding—indeed, a science—that would enable one to identify the "law" of a given society without reference to disputed evaluative questions about the justice or wisdom of a particular cultural phenomenon: the law posited by human persons for the regulation of society. Positivism is a jurisprudential theory. Natural law theory is not. Natural law theorists investigate how it could be the case that there are moral norms knowable by reason, antecedent to and regulative of, all morally significant human choice, including the choice to lay down—"posit"—this law rather than that.

There can be, and are, some natural law theories of law, or (the same thing) natural law jurisprudential theories. As *jurisprudence*, natural law theories of law treat precisely the same subject matter that is the subject of positivist theories of law: the human i.e., declared posited law, and the conceptual tools, i.e., definitions or concepts—required to identify and describe law as a distinct cultural artifact.

What, then, distinguishes natural law jurisprudence? Here the reader must be referred to the groundbreaking work of the world's leading natural law theorist, John Finnis's *Natural Law and Natural Rights*.[70] In the first chapter, Finnis cogently argues that the selection of what he calls "viewpoint" decisively influences the content of a jurisprudential theory, and that viewpoint is dependent upon the theorist's account of genuine human flourishing. Just as a cultural anthropologist must have in mind some notion of the permanent features of human existence, including recurring opportunities for human well-being, so does the legal anthropologist. The challenge to any social scientist, including the jurisprude, is to come up with justified criteria for the formation of general concepts.[71] As Finnis, citing Max Weber, states it, "[d]escriptive social theory . . . cannot in its descriptions do without the concepts found appropriate by men of practical reasonableness to describe to themselves what they think worth doing and achieving. . . ."[72] Finnis concludes that if there is a viewpoint "within which a specifically legal type of social order is presumptively required by practical reason," such a viewpoint is the viewpoint that should be used as the standard of reference by the theorist describing the features of legal order.[73] To put Finnis's point another way, a full-orbed account of genuine human flourishing—a normative point of view—is necessary for the adequate description of law. It is characteristic of legal positivists to deny that proposition.

The set-piece debate between natural lawyers and positivists has been declared over by most of the debaters. Neil MacCormick is a positivist, and he says that "I for one regard the issue of mutual opposition [between natural law and positivism] as now closed and unfruitful." MacCormick points out many "connections" between law and morality. Among them are that certain moral aspirations are intrinsic to law; "the intelligibility of law depends upon . . . moral goods which law and legal institutions secure"; and that legal reasoning is similar to moral reasoning in that both have to do with the question, "what should I do?"

More recently Finnis observed that it is "[b]etter to think there's no such thing as positivism."[74] He added that the truth in legal positivism—seen as a jurisprudential tradition of thought started by Austin and winding through H. L. A. Hart to Joseph Raz—contains nothing that a natural lawyer should deny. And with regard to the important question of what one, all things considered, should actually do, positivism has nothing useful to say. Because the positivists' aim is to clarify the conditions under which a purported legal norm is, according to the rules of that system, "valid," their project is *descriptive*; it is a legal anthropology, as we said above. Positivism is therefore *prescriptively* inert.[75]

NOTES

1. Oliver Wendell Holmes, "The Path of the Law," *Harvard Law Review* 8 (1897): 457, 478.

2. John Finnis, *Natural Law and Natural Rights* (Oxford: Oxford University Press, 1980), 3.

3. See Lon Fuller, *The Morality of Law*, rev. ed. (New Haven, CT: Yale University Press, 1969).

4. For a good discussion of this claim see, e.g., M. H. Kramer, "The Big Bad Wolf: Legal Positivism and Its Detractors," *American Journal of Jurisprudence* 49 (2004): 1.

5. Except for the tendency to promote justice discussed in the text connected to note 4.

6. For more on this doctrine of moral "neutrality," see appendix A.

7. Institutes 1.2.12. Justinian said in the Digest that "since all law is made for the sake of human beings we should speak first of the status of persons." 1.5.2.

8. *Byrn v. New York City Health and Hospitals Corp.*, 286 N.E.2d 887, 889 (N.Y. 1972).

9. *Byrn*, 286 N.E.2d at 889.

10. *Roe v. Wade*, 410 U.S. 113, 159 (1973).

11. Ronald Dworkin, *Law's Empire* (Cambridge, MA: Harvard University Press, 1986), 201.

12. John Rawls, *Political Liberalism* (New York: Columbia University Press, 1993), 243n32.

13. John Calvin Jeffries, *Justice Lewis F. Powell, Jr.* (1994; repr., New York: Fordham University Press, 2001), 350.

14. *Roe*, 410 U.S. at 153, 160–62.

15. David J. Garrow, *Liberty and Sexuality: The Right to Privacy and the Making of "Roe v. Wade"* (New York: Macmillan, 1994), 536–37.

16. Jeffries, *Justice Lewis F. Powell, Jr.,* 350.

17. Ibid.

18. *Baehr v. Lewin*, 852 P.2d 44, 61 (Haw. 1993).

19. *Baehr*, 852 P.2d at 61, 63.

20. *Michael H. v. Gerald D.*, 491 U.S. 110, 141 (1989) (Brennan, J., dissenting).

21. For a discussion of some legitimate ways by which lawmakers should take account of moral pluralism, see appendix B.

22. For a fuller discussion of how law affects culture–and vice versa–see chapter 2.

23. Joseph Raz, *The Morality of Freedom* (New York: Oxford University Press, 1986), 162.

24. Robert P. George, "'Same-Sex Marriage' and 'Moral Neutrality,'" in *Marriage and the Common Good,* ed. K. Whitehead (South Bend, IN: St. Augustine's Press, 2001), 93.

25. See James Madison, *Memorial and Remonstrance against Religious Assessments* (1785), reprinted in the appendix to *Everson v. Board of Education*, 330 U.S. 1, 64 (1947).

26. *Planned Parenthood v. Casey*, 505 U.S. 833, 851 (1992).

27. Hebrews 11:1 (King James Version).

28. *Poe v. Ullman*, 367 U.S. 497, 546 (1961) (Harlan, J., dissenting).

29. *Lawrence v. Texas*, 539 U.S. 558, 574 (2003).

30. *Romer v. Evans*, 517 U.S. 620 (1996).

31. *Lawrence*, 539 U.S. at 582 (O'Connor, J., concurring).

32. *Lawrence*, 539 U.S. at 571 (quoting *Planned Parenthood v. Casey*, 505 U.S. 833, 850 [1992]).

33. The class term for this process of making concrete the more general norms of morality is *determinatio*. For further explanation of this concept, see appendix C.

34. John Finnis, "Natural Law: The Classical Tradition," in *The Oxford Handbook of Jurisprudence and Philosophy of Law*, ed. Jules Coleman and Scott Shapiro (Oxford: Oxford University Press, 2002), 8.

35. Holmes, "The Path of Law," 461.

36. John Finnis, "Law and What I Truly Should Decide," *American Journal of Jurisprudence* 48 (2003): 107, 112.

37. See appendix D for further discussion of how to resolve conflicts within conscience between law and morality.

38. See Marshall Sahlins, *Islands of History* (Chicago: University of Chicago Press, 1985), 104–35.

39. Francis George, "Law and Culture," *Ave Maria Law Review* 1 (2003): 1, 4.

40. See appendix E for a critical look at the assertion "You can't legislate morality."

41. Francis George, "Law and Culture in the United States," *American Journal of Jurisprudence* 48 (2003): 131, 133.

42. *Roe*, 410 U.S. at 113, 153.

43. *Planned Parenthood*, 505 U.S. at 860.

44. *Planned Parenthood*, 505 U.S. at 835.

45. *Brown v. Board of Education*, 347 U.S. 483 (1954).

46. *Plessy v. Ferguson*, 163 U.S. 537 (1896).

47. F. George, "Law and Culture in the United States," 6.

48. See *The Federalist Papers*, ed. Clinton Rossiter (New York: New American Library, 1961), 346.

49. *Everson v. Board of Education*, 330 U.S. 1 (1947).

50. John Courtney Murray, "Law or Prepossessions?" *Law and Contemporary Problems*, 14 (1949): 23.

51. "Oral Argument on Behalf of Appellee Board of Education," from *McCollum v. Board of Education*, 333 U.S. 203, reprinted in *Engage: The Journal of the Federalist Society's Practice Groups* 5 (April 2004): 145.

52. Appendix E includes a review of the famous Hart/Devlin debate over "victimless immoralities."

53. *Regina v. Dudley and Stephens*, 14 Q.B.D. 273 (1884).

54. Justice Anthony M. Kennedy, Speech at the American Bar Association Annual Meeting, August 9, 2003, http://www.supremecourtus.gov/publicinfo/speeches/sp_08-09-03.html.

55. See Exodus 21:24, Leviticus 24:20, and Deuteronomy 19:21. Although typically attributed to Hebrew scripture, the concept also appears prominently in other sources, such as the Code of Hammurabi.

56. H. L. A. Hart, "Prolegomenon to the Principles of Punishment,"

in *Punishment and Responsibility: Essays in the Philosophy of Law* (New York: Oxford University Press, 1968), 1, 8.

57. See Thomas Hobbes, *On the Citizen*, trans. and ed. Richard Tuck and Michael Silverthorne (Cambridge: Cambridge University Press, 1998), 26–31. (Originally published in Latin in 1642 as *De Cive*).

58. Punishment may appropriately include an order of restitution to a person specifically harmed by a given criminal act, but any such specific harm is in addition to that caused to society at large.

59. Robert P. George, "'Same-Sex Marriage' and 'Moral Neutrality,'" in *Marriage and the Common Good* , ed. K. Whitehead (South Bend, IN: St. Augustine's Press, 2001), 83.

60. Ibid. (Much of the next few paragraphs follows Professor George's argument.)

61. Ibid.

62. *Griswold v. Connecticut*, 381 U.S. 479 (1965).

63. *Griswold*, 381 U.S. at 480–83.

64. Robert P. George, *Making Men Moral: Civil Liberties and Public Morality* (New York: Oxford University Press, 1993), 1.

65. See the cogent analysis of the debate in chapter 2 of R. George, *Making Men Moral* (1993).

66. Report of the Committee on Homosexual Offenses and Prostitution (1957), as quoted in R. George, *Making Men Moral*, 49n18.

67. Patrick Devlin, *The Enforcement of Morals* (New York: Oxford University Press, 1965), 14.

68. H. L. A. Hart, *Law, Liberty and Morality*, (Stanford, CA: Stanford University Press, 1963), 50–52.

69. Devlin, *The Enforcement of Morals*, 89n67.

70. Finnis, *Natural Law and Natural Rights*, 3–22.

71. Ibid., 18.

72. Ibid., 16.

73. Ibid., 15.

74. Finnis, "Law and What I Truly Should Decide," *American Journal of Jurisprudence* 48 (2003): 127.

75. Ibid., 129.

BIBLIOGRAPHIC ESSAY

BY CORY L. ANDREWS[*]

❧

READERS MAY WISH TO REFER to several other works to complement the present guide as introductions to jurisprudence: David M. Adams's *Philosophical Problems in the Law* (Wadsworth, 2004), Andrew Altman's *Arguing about Law: An Introduction to Legal Philosophy* (Wadsworth, 2000), Stephen J. Burton's *An Introduction to Law and Legal Reasoning* (Aspen, 1995), and Joel Feinberg and Jules Coleman's *Philosophy of Law* (Wadsworth, 2003). The historical development of the law in human societies is carefully retold in Sir Henry Sumner Maine's classic *Ancient Law* (Oxford University Press, 1927) and John M. Zane's more accessible, but slightly idiosyncratic, *The Story of Law* (Washburn, 1928), the latter released recently in a new edition edited by Charles Reid (Liberty Fund, 1998). Harold Berman persuasively argues for the existence of a cohesive Western legal tradition from the eleventh century to the

---

[*] *Cory L. Andrews received his J.D.* magna cum laude *in 2005 from the University of Florida College of Law, where he served as editor in chief of the* Florida Law Review. *He currently is a law clerk to the Honorable Steven D. Merryday, United States District Court, in Tampa, Florida.*

present in *Law and Revolution: The Formation of the Western Legal Tradition* (Harvard University Press, 1983). Despite these rewarding primers, the beginning student of jurisprudence should spend the majority of his time with the primary rather than the secondary texts, with philosophers of law rather than with books about legal philosophy.

Historically, the antagonism between natural law theory and legal positivism has provided the essential tension in jurisprudence. Acknowledging the necessary overlap of law and morality, natural law theory views the law as resting upon a natural moral order—principles and standards both accessible to human reason and reflecting the moral order of the universe. Augustine of Hippo and Thomas Aquinas are considered the earliest, most articulate proponents of natural law theory. "Because the eternal law is the plan of government in the Chief Governor," Aquinas observed in his *Summa Theologica*, "all the plans of government in the inferior governors must be derived from the eternal law. If at any point [the human law] deflects from the law of nature, it is no longer a law but a perversion of law."

A similarly harmonious view of law and morality was later expounded in the great common law tradition represented by Sir Edward Coke's *Institutes of the Laws of England* (1624–44), William Blackstone's *Commentaries on the Laws of England* (1765–69), Joseph Story's *Commentaries on the Constitution of the United States* (1833), and Justice Samuel Chase's famous Supreme Court opinion in *Calder v. Bull* (1798). For a masterful exploration of natural law's formative role in the development of Anglo-American jurisprudence, see historian Daniel Boorstin's *The Mysterious Science of the Law* (Harvard University Press, 1941). James R. Stoner thoroughly explores the common law tradition in *Common Law and Liberal Theory: Coke, Hobbes, and the Origins of American Constitutionalism* (University Press of Kansas, 1994).

In recent years, a great revival of interest in natural law theory has spread throughout the disciplines. In legal philosophy, this revival was led primarily by John Finnis, whose groundbreaking *Natural Law and Natural Rights* (Oxford University Press, 1980) sparked a debate that continues to rage more than a quarter century later. In addition, Professor Robert P. George's worthy contributions continue to enrich the scholarly literature on natural law theory; see his *Making Men Moral: Civil Liberties and Public Morality* (Oxford University Press, 1993), *Natural Law Theory: Contemporary Essays* (Oxford University Press, 1994), and *In Defense of Natural Law* (Oxford University Press, 2001). Also of interest are Russell Hittinger's *A Critique of the New Natural Law Theory* (University of Notre Dame Press, 1989) and J. Budziszewski's *Written on the Heart: The Case for Natural Law* (InterVarsity Press, 1997). Those seeking a deeper familiarity with the ongoing debate about natural law should consult Edward McLean's *Common Truths: New Perspectives on Natural Law* (ISI Books, 2000), an excellent collection of thoughtful essays by several prominent scholars.

In contrast to natural law, legal positivism views the law as merely a system of orders or commands enforced by some dominant power, usually a sovereign. Under this view, law—more "artificial" than "natural"—represents a purely human contrivance "posited" by an all-powerful lawgiver. Legal positivism emerged as a distinct legal philosophy in the late eighteenth and early nineteenth centuries in the writings of the English philosophers Jeremy Bentham and John Stuart Mill. In his *A Fragment on Government* (1776), Bentham sharply distinguished the mere accurate description of what the law "is" from the normative evaluation of the "rightness" of the law. Bentham described this essential separation of law and morality as the great "utilitarian distinction."

Strongly influenced by Bentham—and by Thomas Hobbes's *Leviathan* (1651)—the English jurist John Austin provided the earliest, most comprehensive account of legal positivism in his landmark work *The Province of Jurisprudence Determined* (1832). "The existence of law is one thing; its merit or demerit is another," Austin proclaimed in a bare-knuckled assault on natural law theory. "Whether it be or be not is one enquiry; whether it be or be not conformable to an assumed standard, is a different enquiry. A law, which actually exists, is a law, though we happen to dislike it, or though it vary from the text, by which we regulate our approbation and disapprobation." For Austin, a proper view of the law is necessarily divorced from any consideration of morality or justice; the law's "ought" must forever be severed from its "is."

Building upon Austin's basic framework, H. L. A. Hart's *The Concept of Law* (Oxford University Press, 1961) undertook to defend legal positivism from criticism while carefully qualifying some of Austin's bolder pronouncements. Hart suggested, among other things, that critics of legal positivism often equate the utilitarian distinction (the insistence on the separation of legality and morality) with Austin's command theory of law (the claim that all law derives from an all-powerful sovereign), resulting in the mistaken conclusion that the latter's vulnerability to criticism somehow indicts the former. Hart insisted that one may logically adhere both to the utilitarian distinction and to utilitarian morality while roundly rejecting Austin's command theory—a position Hart himself adopted.

Elsewhere, in his "Positivism and the Separation of Law and Morals" (*Harvard Law Review* 71 [1958]: 593 ff.), Hart reluctantly acknowledged a kernel of truth in natural law theory. Describing his own view as "soft positivism," Hart conceded the need for a legal code with *some* minimal moral content. For example, Hart agreed that legal prohibitions against physical violence are absolutely essential, not to qualify those prohibitions as "law" but to protect against human vulnerability and to permit civil society to function. Nevertheless, Hart emphasized that one must not unnecessarily conflate the utilitarian need for such laws with the very essence of law itself.

Of course, H. L. A. Hart is otherwise known for his famous midcentury debate with the British jurist Lord

Gerard V. Bradley

Patrick Devlin. The debate, perhaps the opening salvo in today's culture wars, surrounded the Wolfenden Committee's 1957 report recommending the decriminalization of prostitution and homosexual sodomy in England. Insisting that every society must enjoy a shared body of moral values—a "public morality"—Lord Devlin defended the legal enforcement of taboos commonly held by ordinary people. In defending his position, Devlin analogized public morality to the deliberation of a jury. Just as a jury must reach a unanimous decision after calm and careful deliberation, so too must a society overwhelmingly condemn a behavior before legally proscribing it. Hart fervently disagreed, insisting that a society's morality, even if universally held, merits no particular respect from the law. Echoing Bentham and Mill, Hart argued that an individual's conduct may be prohibited only if that conduct is harmful to another, thereby substituting his own utilitarian morality for that of society. Lord Devlin's position in the Hart-Devlin debate is forcefully argued in his *The Enforcement of Morals* (Oxford University Press, 1965). Hart's vigorous criticisms of Devlin's position are set forth in *Law, Liberty, and Morality* (Stanford University Press, 1963). The debate is brilliantly reconsidered in Robert George's "Social Cohesion and the Legal Enforcement of Morals: A Reconsideration of the Hart-Devlin Debate" (*American Journal of Jurisprudence* 35 [1990]: 15 ff.), and Russell Hittinger's "The Hart-Devlin Debate Revisited" (*American Journal of Jurisprudence* 35 [1990]: 47 ff.).

For the definitive intellectual biography of Hart, including an in-depth treatment of his debate with Devlin, see Nicola Lacey's *The Life of H. L. A. Hart: The Nightmare and the Noble Dream* (Oxford University Press, 2004). Leading legal philosophers discuss Hart's response to his critics in Jules Coleman's *Hart's Postscript: Essays on the Postscript to the Concept of Law* (Oxford University Press, 2001). For a scholarly apologia on legal positivism's influence on American law, see Anthony J. Sebok's *Legal Positivism in American Jurisprudence* (Cambridge University Press, 1998). Alternatively, several formidable criticisms of legal positivism are assembled in Robert P. George's *The Autonomy of Law: Essays on Legal Positivism* (Oxford University Press, 1999). Echoes of Lord Devlin's argument for a shared public morality are heard in Harry M. Clor's underappreciated *Public Morality and Liberal Society* (University of Notre Dame Press, 1996).

The work of the late Harvard professor Lon Fuller, though stopping shy of embracing natural law theory, acknowledges that "law" and "what is morally right" are often inseparable. For example, in his *The Morality of Law* (Yale University Press, 1965), Fuller criticizes legal positivism for its apparent inability to explain the ideal of fidelity to law. Although Fuller concedes that an immoral law is nevertheless "law," he expresses doubt that such a law could remain in force for very long if attached to a corrupt and unjust legal system. Kenneth Winston's edited collection, *The Principles of Social Order: Selected Essays of Lon L. Fuller*

(Duke University Press, 1981), provides further insight into Fuller's thought.

In fin de siècle America, legal philosophers began insisting that the actual written laws themselves, whether natural or posited, were ultimately irrelevant. This "rule skepticism," which came to be known as American legal realism, is perhaps best identified with Oliver Wendell Holmes Jr.'s famous essay "The Path of the Law" (1897). Holmes sought to wash the law in "cynical acid"—to reduce it to its bare essentials by tearing down all the ornate drapery of tradition. Holmes insisted that the law must be viewed amorally from the perspective of his prototypical "bad man," a cynic whose only concern is self-gain and self-preservation. Holmes claimed that a plausible legal argument can be constructed to justify any conclusion: "You can give any conclusion a logical form. You can always imply a condition in a contract. But why do you imply it?" Dismissing the role of stare decisis, Holmes maintained that the logically deductive quality of legal reasoning is essentially a myth created by judges who ultimately decide cases largely on the basis of personal policy preferences.

Other influential primary works of American legal realism include Karl Llewellyn, *Bramble Bush: On Our Law and Its Study* (Oceana, 1951); Jerome Frank, *Courts on Trial: Myth and Reality in American Justice* (Princeton University Press, 1973); and Thurman Arnold, *The Symbols of Government* (Oxford University Press, 1948). Typical of the cynicism inherent in American legal realism, Jerome Frank famously claimed that one might accurately predict a judicial outcome by ascertaining what the judge ate for breakfast. For a thorough introduction to American legal realism, see William Fisher, Morton J. Horowitz, and Thomas Reed's *American Legal Realism* (Oxford University Press, 1993), an excellent collection of primary sources and scholarly commentaries. For two fair but devastating critiques of Oliver Wendell Holmes Jr., see Albert W. Alschuler's *Law Without Values: The Life, Work, and Legacy of Justice Holmes* (University of Chicago Press, 2002) and G. Edward White's *Justice Oliver Wendell Holmes: Law and the Inner Self* (Oxford University Press, 1993).

In recent years, the Oxford legal philosopher Ronald Dworkin has articulated one of the most widely debated theories of law. Dworkin argues that the "law" in any given case consists not merely of positive rules but encompasses all the principles and ideals that inform the soundest interpretation of those rules. In Dworkin's view, a court is obliged to adhere to that interpretation of the law which manifests the principles and values of a given community in the most cohesive and morally attractive light. However, Dworkin emphasizes that judges are not bound by moral or normative principles derived from a natural moral order, but may only recognize moral principles that are implicitly or explicitly "present" in the legal history and tradition of their communities. Some of Dworkin's more influential works include *Taking Rights Seriously* (Harvard University Press, 1977); *Law's Empire* (Harvard University Press, 1986); *Life's*

Dominion (Knopf, 1993); and *Sovereign Virtue: The Theory and Practice of Equality* (Harvard University Press, 2002). A collection of scholarly criticisms of Dworkin's theory, with a response from Dworkin, is provided by Justine Burley's *Dworkin and His Critics: With Replies by Dworkin* (Blackwell, 2004).

For cogent criticisms of modern liberal legal theory as best exemplified by John Rawls's *A Theory of Justice* (Harvard University Press, 1971), see George P. Grant's *English Speaking Justice* (Notre Dame Press, 1985), Robert P. George's *Clash of Orthodoxies: Law, Religion, and Morality in Crisis* (ISI Books, 2001), and Robert Bork's *Slouching Towards Gomorrah: Modern Liberalism and American Decline* (Regan Books, 1996). Several centuries of legal philosophy are thoughtfully pondered in Steven D. Smith's *Law's Quandary* (Harvard University Press, 2004), which laments the demise of classical ontological commitments in modern jurisprudence. Finally, the beginning student contemplating the moral foundations of the law simply must read, and reread, Arthur Allen Leff's "Unspeakable Ethics, Unnatural Law" (*Duke Law Journal* [1979]: 1229 ff.).

THE UNITED STATES CONSTITUTION remains the oldest written national constitution in force in the world today. Next to, of course, the text of the Constitution, the obvious place to commence a disciplined study of the ideas undergirding the Constitution is with Alexander Hamilton,

John Jay, and James Madison's *The Federalist* (1788), especially the critical "Gideon" edition edited by George W. Carey and James McClellan (Liberty Fund, 2001). Equally important but often neglected are the influential papers of the Constitution's opponents, the Anti-Federalists, conveniently collected in Herbert Storing's *The Anti-Federalist* (University of Chicago Press, 1985), an abridgment of his magnificent seven-volume *The Complete Anti-Federalist* (University of Chicago Press, 1981).

Additional primary sources can provide the local color and context necessary to appreciate the prevailing worldview of the American founders. For an invaluable clause-by-clause supplement to the Constitution, see Philip B. Kurland and Ralph Lerner's ambitious five-volume collection of debates, letters, papers, and other primary sources, *The Founders' Constitution* (Liberty Fund, 2000). In a similar vein, Charles S. Hyneman and Donald S. Lutz's two-volume *American Political Writing during the Founding Era* (Liberty Press, 1983) provides a fascinating mix of speeches, pamphlets, sermons, and essays gathered from the latter half of the eighteenth century. Every serious student or scholar of the Constitution should own Thurston Greene's *The Language of the Constitution: A Sourcebook and Guide to the Ideas, Terms, and Vocabulary Used by the Framers of the United States Constitution* (Greenwood Press, 1991). As for secondary works on the constitutional era, the evolution of American political and constitutional thought is skillfully delineated in Bernard Bailyn's *The Ideological*

Gerard V. Bradley

Origins of the American Revolution (Belknap Press, 1967); Forrest McDonald's *Novus Ordo Seclorum: The Intellectual Origins of the Constitution* (University Press of Kansas, 1985); and Gordon S. Wood's *The Creation of the American Republic, 1776–1787* (University of North Carolina Press, 1969). The important debate between the Federalists and Anti-Federalists is fully examined in Samuel Beer's *To Make a Nation: The Rediscovery of American Federalism* (Harvard University Press, 1993), M. E. Bradford's *A Better Guide than Reason: Federalists and Anti-Federalists* (Transaction, 1994), and Herbert Storing's *What the Anti-Federalists Were For: The Political Thought of the Opponents of the Constitution* (University of Chicago Press, 1981).

Constitutional interpretation occupies a prominent place in American constitutional theory. As a result, today's constitutional scholarship consists of a cacophony of voices, each of which proclaims its own self-anointed interpretation of the same legal document. This was not always the case. Joseph Story's exhaustive *A Familiar Exposition of the Constitution of the United States* (Harper Bros., 1859) rewards the diligent student with a faithful and reliable exegesis of the Constitution by a leading nineteenth-century legal mind unhampered by today's fashionable academic theories. Among current legal scholars, Keith Whittington has penned two of the most sophisticated and intellectually honest works on constitutional interpretation: *Constitutional Interpretation: Textual Meaning, Original Intent, and Judicial Review* (University Press of Kansas, 1999); and

Constitutional Construction: Divided Powers and Constitutional Meaning (Harvard University Press, 2001). In his masterful defense of "textualism," *A Matter of Interpretation: Federal Courts and the Law* (Princeton University Press, 1997), Justice Antonin Scalia offers an unparalleled original contribution to constitutional scholarship. Historian Johnathan O'Neill's little-known *Originalism in American Law and Politics: A Constitutional History* (John Hopkins University Press, 2005) provides a first-rate intellectual history of originalism as a long-standing, venerable theory of constitutional interpretation. M. E. Bradford unpacks the ideas undergirding the Constitution in *Original Intentions: On the Making and Ratification of the United States Constitution* (University of Georgia Press, 1993).

THE AMERICAN FOUNDERS FEARED judicial activism, the judiciary's usurpation of democratic and legislative functions, as a serious threat to the American experiment of self-governance. In recent decades, those fears increasingly have been confirmed by a Supreme Court bent on "enlightened" social and political change. Among the earliest to sound the warning bell was Alexander Bickel, whose *The Least Dangerous Branch: The Supreme Court at the Bar of Politics* (Bobbs-Merrill Co., 1962) remains a seminal book on the excesses of Supreme Court power. Other prescient voices have followed, including John Agresto, *The Supreme Court and Constitutional Democracy* (Cornell University Press,

1984); Raoul Berger, *Government by Judiciary* (Liberty Fund, 1997); Robert Bork, *Coercing Virtue: The Worldwide Rule of Judges* (AEI Press, 2003); Larry Kramer, *The People Themselves: Popular Constitutionalism and Judicial Review* (Oxford University Press, 2006); Richard John Neuhaus, *The End of Democracy? The Celebrated* First Things *Debate* (Spence, 1997); and Christopher Wolfe, *The Rise of Modern Judicial Review* (Rowman & Littlefield, 1994).

Additional edifying works on American constitutional law include Hadley Arkes, *Beyond the Constitution* (Princeton University Press, 1992); Raoul Berger, *Selected Writings on the Constitution* (James River Press, 1987); Walter Berns, *Taking the Constitution Seriously* (Madison Books, 1987); Sotirios Barber and Robert P. George, *Constitutional Politics: Essays on Constitution Making, Maintenance, and Change* (Princeton University Press, 2001); A. V. Dicey, *Introduction to the Study of the Law of the Constitution* (Liberty Fund, 1982); Robert P. George, *Great Cases in Constitutional Law* (Princeton University Press, 2000); Edward B. McLean, *Derailing the Constitution* (ISI Books, 1995); Stephen B. Presser, *Recapturing the Constitution: Race, Religion, and Abortion Reconsidered* (Regnery Publishing, 1994); and James R. Stoner, *Common Law Liberty: Rethinking American Constitutionalism* (University Press of Kansas, 2003).

The discerning reader will benefit from Robert Bork's recent *A Country I Do Not Recognize* (Hoover Press, 2005), an engaging collection of essays chronicling the ongoing legal assault on American values. Steven D. Smith provides a wide-ranging philosophic overview of the entire constitutional project in his iconoclastic *The Constitution and the Pride of Reason* (Oxford University Press, 1998), a heady but rewarding read. For an intelligent discussion of federalism, one need look no further than Martin Diamond's collection of brilliant essays, *As Far as Republican Principles Will Admit* (AEI Press, 1992). Finally, Mary Ann Glendon provides a welcome antidote to America's rights-laden political discourse with her widely-praised *Rights Talk: The Impoverishment of Political Discourse* (Free Press, 1991).

———

DISSENTING IN *Terminiello v. City of Chicago* in 1949, Justice Jackson observed, "There is danger that, if the Court does not temper its doctrinaire logic with a little practical wisdom, it will convert the constitutional Bill of Rights into a suicide pact." Responding to the libertarian triumphalism of the majority's opinion, Jackson argued that Terminiello's hate-filled public rant crossed the bounds of civilized speech, posed a legitimate threat to public order, and was undeserving of constitutional protection. In recent years, many civil libertarians have exalted the freedom of speech above any other competing constitutional consideration. For a more balanced and sensible view of the speech protections afforded by the First Amendment, see Harry M. Clor's *Obscenity and Public Morality: Censorship in a Liberal Society* (University of Chicago Press, 1969),

Rochelle Gurstein's *The Repeal of Reticence* (Hill & Wang, 1996), David Lowenthal's *No Liberty for License: The Forgotten Logic of the First Amendment* (Spence, 1997), Kevin Saunders's *Saving Our Children from the First Amendment* (NYU Press, 2004), and Walter Berns's *The First Amendment and the Future of Democracy* (Regnery, 1985). Professor Eugene Volokh formidably defends the libertarian view of free speech in his popular casebook *The First Amendment and Related Statutes: Problems, Cases and Policy Arguments* (Foundation Press, 2005).

THE SUPREME COURT'S CONTROVERSIAL 1973 decision in *Roe v. Wade* met with blistering academic criticism, including from those who championed legalized abortion. John Hart Ely's devastating article, "The Wages of Crying Wolf: A Comment on *Roe v. Wade*" (*Yale Law Journal* 82 [1973]: 920 ff.), summed up the view of many: "It is bad because it is bad law, or rather because it is *not* constitutional law and gives almost no sense of an obligation to try to be." The academic consensus that *Roe* is a legal and logical disaster is so overwhelming that leading scholars have undertaken to rewrite the decision in Jack Balkin's *What* Roe v. Wade *Should Have Said: The Nation's Top Legal Experts Rewrite America's Most Controversial Decision* (NYU Press, 2005).

For now, the issue of abortion remains at the white-hot center of American politics. Of course, if the Supreme

Court overturned *Roe v. Wade* tomorrow, it would not result in the prohibition of so much as a single abortion. Abortion policy simply would return to the people of the fifty states and their democratically elected representatives, where it had resided throughout most of this nation's history. Two distinctly different approaches to Americans' history with abortion before *Roe* are presented in Marvin Olasky's *Abortion Rites: A Social History of Abortion in America* (Regnery, 1992) and James C. Mohr's *Abortion in America: The Origins and Evolution of National Policy* (Oxford University Press, 1979). For a thorough and even-handed introduction to *Roe v. Wade*, see N. E. Hull and Peter Charles Hoffer's Roe v. Wade: *The Abortion Rights Controversy in American History* (University Press of Kansas, 2001). An insightful comparative approach to the issue of abortion is provided in the relevant portions of Mary Ann Glendon's *Abortion and Divorce in Western Law* (Harvard University Press, 1989). Judge Richard Posner predictably articulates the libertarian view of privacy and morality in his *Sex and Reason* (Harvard University Press, 2004), while Laurence Tribe's *Abortion: The Clash of Absolutes* (W. W. Norton, 1992) presents a comprehensive and sympathetic view of legalized abortion. Rigorous philosophical critiques of abortion are presented in Hadley Arkes's *Natural Rights and the Right to Choose* (Cambridge University Press, 2002) and Peter Kreeft's *Three Approaches to Abortion* (Ignatius, 2002).

Gerard V. Bradley

THE FIRST AMENDMENT PROVIDES in part, "Congress shall make no law respecting an establishment of religion or prohibiting the free exercise thereof." These sixteen words, which include the "Establishment Clause" and the "Free Exercise Clause" (known together as the Constitution's religion clauses), have been a great source of confusion throughout much of the nation's history. For the student desiring deeper familiarity with this history, historian James Hitchcock's two-volume *The Supreme Court and Religion in American Life* (Princeton University Press, 2004) provides a lively and meticulously researched account of the Supreme Court's religion jurisprudence. Additionally, the novice seeking a general orientation to the scholarly debates on this subject will benefit from Stephen M. Feldman's *Law and Religion: A Critical Anthology* (NYU Press, 2000), which presents a wide range of academic perspectives.

Inextricably bound to any discussion of the constitutional role of religion in American life is the ubiquitous cry to fortify the "wall of separation between church and state." Of course, this metaphor, which first appeared in a once-obscure 1802 letter of Thomas Jefferson to the Danbury Baptist Association, appears nowhere in the Constitution. Phillip Hamburger's magnificent *The Separation of Church and State* (Harvard University Press, 2002) presents the definitive intellectual history of America's obsession with "separationism" and will reshape the legal and scholarly debate for years to come. Likewise, Robert L. Cord's pithy

Separation of Church and State: Historical Fact and Current Fiction (Carlson Publishing, 1982) continues to reward all who read it.

Many excellent works address the intellectual incoherence of the Supreme Court's recent religion jurisprudence, which scholars of all philosophical stripes agree is hopelessly muddled. The best of these include Gerard Bradley's *Church-State Relationships in America* (Greenwood Press, 1987), John Witte's *Religion and the American Constitutional Experiment: Essential Rights and Liberties* (Westview Press, 1999), and Michael McConnell's superb casebook, *Religion and the Constitution* (Aspen Publishers, 2002). One especially thought-provoking treatment is Steven D. Smith's *Foreordained Failure: The Quest for a Constitutional Principle of Religious Freedom* (Oxford University Press, 1995), which argues that the present conundrum unavoidably results from the inherent limitations of constitutional interpretation.

For a uniquely Christian perspective on these issues, the aptly named *Christian Perspectives on Legal Thought* (Yale University Press, 2001) provides an eclectic collection of essays assembled by Michael McConnell, Robert Cochran Jr., and Angela Carmella on the legal status of religious faith in American society. A decidedly Catholic approach is set forth in John Courtney Murray's *Religious Liberty: Catholic Struggles with Pluralism* (Westminster John Knox Press, 1993). And last, but hardly least, religion's proper place in American public life is thoughtfully considered in an essay that should be read by all students: Wilfred McClay's indispensable "Two Concepts of Secularism" (*Wilson Quarterly* 24, no. 3 [Summer 2000]: 54), which appears also in the excellent *Religion Returns to the Public Square* (Johns Hopkins University Press, 2003), edited by Wilfred McClay and Hugh Heclo.

INTERCOLLEGIATE STUDIES INSTITUTE

think. live free.™

ISI Books is the publishing imprint of the
Intercollegiate Studies Institute.

Most thoughtful college students are sick of getting
a shallow education in which too many viewpoints
are shut out and rigorous discussion is shut down.

We teach them the principles of liberty and plug
them into a vibrant intellectual community so that
they get the collegiate experience they hunger for.

join.isi.org